AN INTRODUCTION TO

ATTRIBUTION PROCESSES

Kelly G. Shaver

The College of William and Mary

LEA LAWRENCE ERLBAUM ASSOCIATES, PUBLISHERS
1983   Hillsdale, New Jersey   London

Lawrence Erlbaum Associates, Inc., Publishers
365 Broadway
Hillsdale, New Jersey 07642

Library of Congress Cataloging in Publication Data

Shaver, Kelly G   1941-
   An introduction to attribution processes.

   Bibliography: p.
   1. Social perception.   2. Interpersonal relations.
I. Title. [DNLM: 1. Behavior.   2. Character.
BF199 S533i]
HM132.S49   301.11   74-23663
ISBN 0-89859-351-4

Printed in the United States of America
10 9 8 7 6 5 4 3 2 1

To Carole and Vicky

CONTENTS

PREFACE

Why do people act the way they do? How do their desires and fears become known to us? When are our opinions of others correct, and when are they likely to be mistaken? These are questions which attribution theory tries to answer. We are not content merely to observe the behavior of others; we also want to understand it. Specifically, we need to explain actions that occur, and we need to be able to predict when they are likely to recur in the future. The principles of attribution theory show one way in which this search for meaning in human behavior might proceed.

In our everyday lives we are not dispassionate observers of human behavior, watching without evaluation. On the contrary, we try to understand behavior, to explain it, to determine what it means for us, and to make value judgments about it. Is another person complimenting me because I have behaved admirably, or is he flattering me because I have something he wants? Does the aspiring politician really believe his own campaign slogans, or is he simply taking positions he thinks will be popular with the voters? Is a particular criminal defendant to be held personally responsible for a crime, or were there extenuating circumstances that might serve as justification for the action? In each of these cases our main interest is not in the action, but rather in the presumed reasons behind the action. In short, to what should each of these behaviors be attributed?

Understanding human action is not only the objective of social science, it is also the goal of ordinary people. This book provides a thorough introduction to the field of attribution, but the theoretical principles and issues are illustrated primarily with everyday examples. No attempt is made to present a comprehensive review of experimental research; those studies that are included have been chosen for their explanatory value. Because of its informal approach, this book should interest all readers with a desire to increase their understanding of the causes of human behavior.

Although I must bear the responsibility for any weaknesses that remain in the book, a number of people deserve mention for their contributions to its development. My interest in attribution processes was first sparked under the guidance of Edward E. Jones, and the book reflects many of his ideas. I have also drawn extensively on the work of Fritz Heider and Harold H. Kelley, and I am indebted to all three men for their review and criticism of portions of the manuscript, particularly in Chapter 4. I am especially indebted to Stan Evans of Winthrop Publishers, whose enthusiasm, ideas, and support were invaluable to the completion of the manuscript. The helpful comments of Lloyd K. Stires and Stephen C. Jones identified weaknesses in earlier drafts of the book. I am particularly grateful to Lloyd Stires for his painstaking and excellent criticism of the entire manuscript. Thanks are also due my students, especially Lee Hamilton and Patricia Hays, for helping to identify ambiguities and excessive use of jargon. Finally, a special word of appreciation is due my wife, Carole, for her critical reading, for typing the manuscript, and for her continued interest and support throughout the undertaking.

1

INTRODUCTION

How are people's actions to be interpreted and understood? What are the underlying regularities in another's personality? How does the social environment affect even the perception of one's own behavior? The purpose of this book is to introduce you to an area of social psychology—attribution—that describes the processes by which these inferences may be made. Much of the social behavior of individuals, groups, and even nations is affected by the capabilities and desires that are attributed to friends and adversaries alike. Indeed, friendship itself is something that we infer from the behavior of other people: if a person says pleasant words to you, offers to help you with tasks that you must perform, provides support for you when you are feeling low, is happy when you are, then you will most probably consider that person a friend. You have evaluated the person's behavior as positive toward you, determined that he has nothing of great value to gain by currying your favor, and may have observed that he does not behave in the same way with just everybody. In other words, you have made an attribution to the person of friendliness toward you as a social object.

The pages that follow will describe the basic processes involved in the attribution of such underlying dispositions, will present some of the situational factors and personal motives that may influence attribution, and will show some of the interpersonal consequences of our attempts to understand the meaning of human action. We begin with two examples which illustrate important principles of attribution and suggest why they might be worth study.

Perceivers, Attributions, and Dispositions

The Cuban missile crisis of 1962 is an excellent example, on a national level, of the importance of attributed intentions and motives.

In a televised address to the nation, President John F. Kennedy confirmed rumors that Russia had begun to install intermediate-range ballistic missiles into shielded bunkers in Cuba. Throughout the succeeding weeks, the Soviet Union maintained that the missiles were for purely defensive purposes and were being installed at the request of the newly established Cuban government of Fidel Castro. For a number of reasons, however, the prevailing view in this country was that the missiles (which had sufficient range to reach most of North and South America) would be used for "nuclear blackmail" of pro–United States governments in Central and South America. At that time most Americans considered their country to be moral and peace-loving,* and since there was little general knowledge of the intent behind the CIA-directed invasion of Cuba (the ill-fated Bay of Pigs operation), the assertion that these missiles were only for defensive purposes had little influence on American public opinion. Moreover, those were the cold war days, before the Sino-Soviet split, when most Americans perceived Communism to be a monolithic, expansionist movement—a view reinforced by actions such as Russia's crushing the rebellion of the Hungarian freedom fighters six years earlier. Finally, the new president was a liberal Democrat whom some considered to be less concerned about containing the spread of Communism than was his Republican predecessor. As a result of these and other factors, the presence of the missiles was generally thought to represent a direct threat to the security of the United States. In the language of attribution theory, the *action* (installing the missiles) was *attributed to* an *underlying disposition* (belligerence toward the United States). Thus, the action was considered to be not an isolated instance of behavior with no implications for the future, but rather a manifestation of a stable disposition that would probably give rise to other threatening actions in the future.

This example shows that persons are seldom content to be passive observers of behavior. Rather they are active perceivers of action, engaged in a search for the regularities underlying the behavior they observe, and their very activity will have consequences for the attributions that they will make. To no small degree the disposition inferred from an action is in the eye of the perceiver: while nations friendly to the United States joined in expressing their indignation, nations friendly to the Soviet Union publicly wondered what all the fuss was about. Not only can a perceiver's viewpoint help shape the nature of a disposition inferred from behavior, it can affect the relative importance assigned to that disposition. The United States

---

*For a more recent examination of the consequences of this self-image, see White, 1970.

and other countries within range of the missiles were certainly more upset by the imputed belligerence than were those of their allies who were out of range.

The persistent search for the meaning of behavior, and the effects of the active involvement of the perceiver, can also be seen in situations much less extreme than the national crisis of our first example. Consider for a moment the task facing a jury in the criminal trial of a person accused of assault. Testimony has established that the defendant was arguing with a shopkeeper over the price of an article that was supposed to be on sale. As the argument became more heated, the shopkeeper attempted to usher the defendant out of the store. Witnesses for both the prosecution and the defense agreed that the defendant refused to move and that the two suddenly came to blows. There was, however, some disagreement about the degree of provocation, and no one could remember with absolute certainty whether the defendant had thrown the first punches. Lengthy cross-examination by both sides has failed to discredit any key witnesses, so the jury is faced with resolving the discrepancy. Again, in the language of attribution, the jury must make an *attribution of causality,* either to a dispositional quality of the actor (a personal disposition) or to a factor in the environment such as provocation by the shopkeeper (an environmental disposition). It should be emphasized that throughout this book the meaning of the term *personal disposition* will be restricted to cases of attribution to the particular actor in question, while the term *environmental disposition* will be used to describe any attribution to factors other than the actor (including, as in the present example, possible provocations from other persons).

It is clear that the defendant's fate depends on the attribution that is made, with a personal attribution leading to a guilty verdict and an environmental attribution (such as justifiable self-defense) leading to acquittal. It is less apparent though equally true that, as in the missile crisis example, the personal characteristics of perceivers (here, the jury) can affect the resulting attribution. To help illustrate the point, evaluate this case for yourself. Without looking back, can you guess the sex and race of the defendant? You probably guessed that the defendant was male and perhaps black. In the absence of any information, this guess is most apt to be correct, since the modal defendant in an assault case is a black male. This perfectly rational guess becomes a personal bias when it serves as an estimate not of the characteristics of the average defendant, but of the guilt or innocence of an individual. Suppose you were informed that the defendant was actually a white, upper-middle-class woman. With all other things equal, would you consider her more likely or less likely to be guilty than a lower-class black male? If yours is a typical response, you would judge the female less likely to be guilty than the male. Rokeach and Vidmar (1973) report data that suggest possible bias against defendants who are lower-class rather than middle- or upper-class, and who are black rather than white. Other research by Landy and Aronson (1969) raises the distinct possibility that there would be bias in favor of a female defendant, especially with a predominantly male jury. Thus, even in situations which emphasize objectivity in interpersonal evaluation, perceivers bring with them attitudes and values that can affect their decisions. The influence of these factors can only be greater on the everyday attributions we make under less well defined and objective circumstances.

The Goals of Attribution: Understanding and Prediction

Both the missile crisis and the jury deliberation examples illustrate a fundamental assumption of attribution theory: perceivers will try to identify the causes of the behavior they observe. Why should this be the case? What can perceivers gain from a dispositional attribution (either to a person or to the environment) that is not inherent in their observation of the action? First, the perceivers can *increase their understanding of the behavior*. We are not satisfied with mere observation of actions, in part because there are just too many such actions for us to keep track of them all. There is a limit to the amount of perceptual information that a human being can comprehend, and through various devices such as selective attention, categorization of stimuli, and attribution of dispositions, perceivers will simplify their worlds to manageable proportions. In this regard, a dispositional attribution provides the common denominator for a variety of actions and serves to organize them into a meaningful pattern. Thus it was not important to American citizens whether the missiles had been moved into Cuba by cargo ship or by barge, during weekdays or on weekends, when the moon was full or when it was new, but simply that they were there and that their presence was viewed as a potentially hostile action. As is the case with other kinds of cognitive categorization, a dispositional attribution may disregard some crucial information (and thereby be incorrect) while permitting the perceivers to attend to those aspects of the situation that appear important to them.

If the first goal of attribution is to increase the perceivers' understanding of the social world around them, the second objective of dispositional attribution is to *increase the perceivers' ability to predict what the actor is likely to do in the future.* If the action taken in either of our examples were thought to be accidental (Russia really intended those missiles to be sent to Albania; the defendant was really just trying to catch himself after slipping on a banana peel), there would be no way for a perceiver to estimate the likelihood that the action would recur in the future. With a dispositional attribution to the environment (threat to the security of Cuba by the United States or provocation by the shopkeeper), the perceiver would begin to expect a similar response to the same conditions in the future. Repetition of the action would then appear to be contingent on future circumstances. Attribution of the action to a personal disposition of the actor, however, would imply that future similar actions might be taken regardless of the circumstances. Here again, because the meaning seen by the perceiver in the action can be incorrect, the prediction based on a dispositional attribution can be faulty. Changes in the environment could overpower the effect of the disposition—the world balance of power could change so that Russia and the United States could find themselves to be allies—or the fact of the attribution could be mistaken. Despite these possibilities for error, it is still probably true that dispositional attribution increases the perceiver's ability to predict future behavior of the actor beyond what would be possible from observation without attribution. The place of these two goals—understanding and prediction—in the attribution process will be more fully discussed in Chapter 3.

The Nature of the Attribution Process: Plan of the Book

Whether the situation makes explicit the problem-solving nature of attribution, as in the case of jury deliberation, or whether the process appears immediate, it nevertheless remains a *process* to which the perceiver has contributed. By virtue of his active participation in his search for the causes and meaning of behavior of others, the perceiver can make (often unconsciously) significant errors in attribution. The remainder of the book outlines the origins of current attribution theory, examines models of the inference process, and suggests some of the interpersonal consequences that can follow the attributions we make.

Although a person's attributions are an important influence on his behavior, they are not his only interpersonal judgments. From a broader perspective, the approach and method of attribution theory owe an intellectual debt to the general area of social psychology known as *person perception*. Chapter 2 acknowledges this debt with an outline of traditional elements of person perception. It illustrates differences between the perception of inanimate objects and the perception of persons, showing how the latter is complicated by the thinking and acting of the stimulus person. Students who already have a solid background in person perception should go directly to Chapter 3, which traces the development of an identifiable body of attribution theory from two earlier research traditions—interest in the characteristics of persons who seem to be highly accurate judges of others, and interest in the influence of bodily needs and personality dynamics on perception. To provide an orientation to the models of attribution that follow, Chapter 3 will conclude with an analysis of the essential stages of the attribution process.

Chapter 4 will begin with the pioneering work of Fritz Heider (1958), then consider the extensions of that theory proposed by Jones and Davis (1965) and Kelley (1967, 1971). The strengths and weaknesses of each of these models of the attribution process will be discussed in Chapter 5, which will show how each model deals with the elements of the attribution process—observation, intention, dispositional attribution. This is a difficult chapter, primarily of value to highly interested students. Since its content is not carried over into the remainder of the book, introductory students may omit the chapter without any loss of continuity.

The next three chapters will consider dispositional attributions to specified individual actors. Chapter 6 will describe attributions that perceivers make for their own behavior, and will discuss the possible reasons for the discrepancies that are often obtained between the descriptions of actors and observers. Chapter 7 will identify the personal and situational determinants of judgments of personal causality and responsibility. Of all the dispositional attributions that a perceiver may make, the attribution of causality to another person is perhaps the most important, if only because other inferences to be made about the stimulus person depend on the belief that his behavior was intended. Following this discussion of the attribution of causality, Chapter 8 will describe the ways in which personality dispositions are inferred from the actor's behavior and the context in which that behavior is performed.

Finally, Chapter 9 will consider how the attributions that a perceiver makes can influence his subsequent behavior toward the stimulus person. Research will be discussed that suggests how a person's behavior toward himself can be altered by changes in attributions made during psychotherapy, and how his actions toward other individuals or groups can depend on his attributions of the causes for their behavior. Of particular interest are the possible consequences of differences between personal and environmental attributions for phenomena as diverse as changes in self-concept, commitment to mental institutions, and domestic social welfare policies.

2

THE FOUNDATION OF ATTRIBUTION: Person Perception

We have seen that perceivers are active participants in the perceptual process: they try to explain and predict human behavior through processes described by attribution theory. At this point you may wonder just where attribution fits in the larger context of social psychology. Is it found in phenomena of socialization? Attitude change? Group dynamics? A case can be made for the importance of attribution in all of these areas, but historically attribution theory is most closely identified with social perception. The basic data for any attribution are, after all, the actions of persons, so in both approach and method, attribution theory has developed out of the area of social psychology known as person perception. You will probably find it easier to understand attribution theory if you are familiar with some of the traditional concerns of person perception, such as models of the process, descriptions of the stimulus, and actions of the person that contribute to the perceiver's impression. Accordingly, this chapter summarizes major elements of person perception. Comprehensive review is beyond the scope of this book; advanced students are referred to detailed discussions by Taguiri and Petrullo (1958) and later by Taguiri (1969).

Social Perception as a Lens of the World

Whether the stimulus for perception is an inanimate object or another person, the result of the perceptual process can be defined, following Allport (1955), as "a phenomenological experience of the object, that is to say, the way some object or situation appears to the subject . . ." (p. 23). It is assumed by this definition that an objective reality which contains both things and people exists outside the perceiver. To indicate that these physical and social objects are remote from the perceiver and cannot be directly experienced by him, they are referred to as *distal objects*. After some appropriate kind of mediation—light waves, sound waves, physical contact—a distal object will become represented at the perceiver's peripheral sense organs. The light waves produce an identifiable pattern on the rods and cones in the retina of the eye, the sound waves stimulate a particular pattern of response by various elements of the inner ear, and the physical contact gives rise to a pattern of response from receptors in the skin that are sensitive to pressure and temperature. In each case, the resulting pattern of stimulation of receptors is called the *proximal stimulus* and is the local and immediate representation of the distal object out in the world. It is generally agreed (see Allport, 1955) that the proximal stimulus is less than perfect as a representation of the distal object; some information is almost necessarily lost, either through selective attention on the part of the perceiver, or through what has been called a limitation in "channel capacity." This refers to the fact that only so much information can be accepted by the sense organs at a particular moment in time, and a complex stimulus can easily overwhelm the capacity of those organs to translate it into nerve impulses. We shall return to this limitation below, in the discussion of categorization.

The proximal stimulus must undergo still further modification before it leads to the final percept. While the stimulation of the receptors is rather faithfully translated into neural firing, that transmission must be evaluated against a background of whatever other neural activity is occurring at the same time. Activity from the presence of organic states in the body such as hunger and thirst, from muscle feedback, and from the general activity of the brain all contribute to a *field* that forms the background for any single proximal stimulus. Although the precise neural mechanisms are not now clear, the field includes not only present stimulation, but also memories of past events and expectancies for the future. Thus, the interpretation of the proximal stimulus can best be considered as a *constructive process,* an integration of sensory input with other ongoing activity.

This view of the perceptual process is best summarized by the "lens model" of Brunswik (1934), shown in Figure 2-1. The mediation between the distal object and the proximal stimulus can be represented by diverging lines, since it is usually the case that the distal object is there for anyone to perceive. If you are listening to recorded music with friends, the sound from the speakers is available to you all (unless you have selfishly put on headphones) and it is

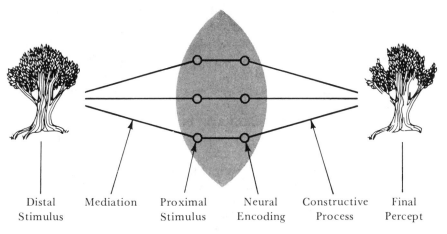

| Distal | Mediation | Proximal | Neural | Constructive | Final |
| Stimulus | | Stimulus | Encoding | Process | Percept |

Figure 2-1. The Brunswik lens model of perception (1934) shows the course of perception from the distal stimulus in the real world to the final percept in the phenomenological world of the perceiver. (Adapted from Heider, 1958.)

up to each one of you to act as a lens for this sensory experience by focusing it into an individual percept of the music. The converging of the lines from neural encoding to the final percept is intended to illustrate that the constructive process within the perceiver is an *active* interpretation of the proximal stimulus rather than a passive and utterly faithful transmission of it. Just as information (and thus accuracy) is lost from distal object to proximal stimulus, still more is lost in the attempt to perceive against an ongoing field of other stimulation. While you may be particularly interested in the sheer loudness of the music, one of your friends may be more attuned to the rhythm, and another may be concentrating on the lyrics. The resulting percept may differ for each of you, even though the proximal stimulation is most probably the same.

Although Brunswik's lens model was first developed to apply to cases of object perception, Heider (1958) adapted it for use in description of social perception as well. A major difference between the two uses is a change in the nature of the mediation. Recall that in the case of object perception, mediation consists entirely of physical entities—light waves, sound waves, temperatures, pressures, and so forth. In contrast, when the distal stimulus is a social object (for example, another person), the perceiver's proximal stimulus corresponding to that person may be derived not from first-hand contact with the person, but rather from a description of the stimulus person made by a third party. This possibility of mediation by a third person will, as a matter of course, increase the likelihood that the proximal stimulus will not be a completely accurate reflection of the distal object. Now the third person's needs, and his attitudes toward the stimulus person, are interposed between the distal object and the proximal stimulus arrived at by the perceiver, and these are bound to affect the quality of the mediation.

There is an additional possibility for error when the distal object is a personal disposition of the actor, as revealed by the actions that he is observed taking. To illustrate this possible source of error in the proximal stimulus, Heider distinguished between what he called *ambiguous* and *synonymous* mediation. If the action is considered to be part of the mediation, then an action that reflects the disposition unequivocally would be considered a synonymous mediation—the action itself is a synonym for the disposition. If, however, the action could reflect any number of possible dispositions, including the one of interest, then the mediation is said to be ambiguous. If a person is observed dashing into a burning building at considerable risk to himself in order to save people trapped inside, that action rather unequivocally reflects a disposition of helpfulness and altruism. If, on the other hand, the same person is observed helping his employer build an addition onto the employer's house, the mediation is ambiguous. It might be the case that the stimulus person is truly helpful, or it might be that he is trying to impress his boss, or it might even be that he is getting practice for some intended additions to his own home. We will return to this problem of uncertainty in conjunction with both correspondent inference theory (Chapter 4) and the discounting principle (Chapter 7).

From this brief look at the lens model, we can see that there are two major elements of the process of social perception that are especially prone to error. First, since many of our social perceptions are screened through the eyes of others rather than experienced first hand, the mediation between the distal object (such as action) and the proximal stimulus (the representation of that action) may be faulty. Second, because of the greater complexity of social stimuli, there is greater potential for distortion during the constructive process.

Unfortunately, it is also more difficult to assess the extent of such errors in social perception than in the perception of physical objects. In the case of physical perception it is relatively easy to measure what Allport (1955) calls *veridicality:* the degree to which the phenomenal experience (percept) agrees with the objective reality (the distal stimulus). A perception that two lines are parallel can readily be compared to objective reality with a ruler and straightedge. While this comparison is itself a series of perceptual judgments, it is relatively simple to obtain quite high degrees of agreement between perceivers about the comparison. A social perception, in contrast, is much less likely to be measurable in purely physical terms, so veridicality must be determined by comparisons among a number of perceivers in the sometimes naive hope that their peculiarities will somehow cancel out.

Social Perception as Categorization

Students of perception have typically distinguished between the perception of inanimate objects and the perception of persons, partially in the belief that person perception is *qualitatively,* as well as quantitatively, different from object perception (Allport, 1955; Taguiri and Petrullo, 1958). The most obvious reason for such a distinction is that the stimulus object in person perception is, like the perceiver, a thinking and feeling person considered capable of intentional action. The victim of a mugging who is trying to identify his assailant from a police line-up is not merely making a perceptual judgment. He is also wondering what consequences that judgment will have, both for his attacker and for himself. Although the victim (the perceiver) may be making his judgment from behind a one-way mirror, he is apt to believe that the attacker may know who is providing such information to the police. If for some reason there is no conviction at a subsequent trial, the perceiver may well be a victim again, this time for the perceptual judgment he has made. This is certainly an extreme example, but it does illustrate the point that the distal stimulus in person perception is a thinking and volitional being capable of providing the perceiver with rewards or punishments contingent on the perceptual judgments that are made.

In addition to being capable of intentional action, the stimulus in person perception is infinitely more complex than the stimulus in object perception. Although this difference could be considered only one of degree, its magnitude has two consequences—the necessity for grouping of elements and the organization of those elements over time—that suggest qualitative differences in the resulting process. As pointed out above, the human perceiver has a limited channel capacity that precludes complete proximal representation of the distal stimulus, even when that stimulus is merely a complex inanimate one. In such cases, and almost always in the case of person perception, the perceiver simply cannot encode all of the discrete elements that make up the stimulus. The result, as Bruner (1957) suggests, is that perception is really best considered an act of *categorization:* through early experiences the perceiver learns what stimulus elements are reliably associated with each other and becomes able to combine these into meaningful categories. Since these categories imply rules for classifying incoming information, perception is seen as a problem-solving task in which the perceiver attempts to decide whether the stimulus person possesses attributes that would place him in any of several appropriate categories.

In making this determination, some aspects of the stimulus person are obviously more relevant than others. For example, a stimulus person's statements about political leaders are probably a pretty good indication of his overall political orientation, but the size of his left earlobe is totally uninformative in this regard. Bruner refers to such relevant attributes as *criterial,* in the sense that together they define the boundaries of the category. Some categories are defined by a single criterial attribute—FBI agent, Democrat, and Lion are categories defined by formal membership in an organization—while other categories have multiple criterial attributes—humanitarian, philanthropist, snob. Within a single category having multiple criterial attributes, some attributes may be more important than others. Philanthropists may vary in their degree of concern for others, but all are characterized by the act of donation.

DIFFICULTIES IN CATEGORIZATION

Given the complexity of social stimuli, some degree of categorization in perception is inevitable, but at the same time there are some well-known problems created by this process; for example, *stereotyping.* Consider for a moment the category "housewife." The criterial attributes of this category usually include being female (although the emergence of the term *house-husband* suggests that this attribute may become less criterial), being married (this, too, may change in time), and engaging in few or no activities or employment outside the home. It is important to notice that while these are the only truly criterial attributes, they are not the only attributes ever found among members of the category. Housewives often have children, sometimes drive station wagons, and occasionally become so wrapped up in their home lives that they lose interest in anything else. Indeed, it is possible that in the experience of a particular perceiver, these additional attributes form the "typical instance" of the category. The perceptually justifiable process of categorization becomes indefensible and potentially dangerous stereotyping if our perceiver applies all attributes, criterial or not, to every new instance of the category with whom he comes in contact. A woman is not necessarily a dull conversationalist just because she drives a station wagon. It is this confusion between the typical instance and the criterial attributes that is the essence of stereotyping.

A related difficulty that can arise in the course of perceptual categorization has been designated by Jones and Gerard (1967) as the *prior entry effect:* early information will have contributed to the formation of the category more than later disconfirmations are likely to contribute to its change. This effect is an acknowledgement of the fact that, in all but the most rigid perceivers, the process of categorization is an interchange between the existing cognitive or perceptual category and new information that is received. When a perceiver is confronted by a social stimulus that is novel in his experience, he has difficulty distinguishing between criterial attributes and other aspects of the stimulus that may be unique to the particular instance. In the absence of a preexisting perceptual pigeonhole, the novel social stimulus creates a new cognitive category. Only interaction with other persons who are members of the category will permit the perceiver to distinguish between criterial and noncriterial attributes, but here the prior entry effect comes into play. The early information has created a perceptual or cognitive category, and that existing category has shaped the later input. The attributes associated with the category act both to screen out relevant information (the perceiver only pays attention to familiar attributes) and then to add to the information provided (once the category designation is chosen, attributes of the typical instance are assumed even if the new stimulus person has not exhibited them). In part because of the cognitive prior entry effect, the attitudes and values formed during early development of categories will be highly resistant to later change. Some of the attributional styles which may be learned in this way, such as internal-external control, are discussed in Chapter 8.

Description of the Stimulus

Person perception can legitimately be considered an active process of categorization, in which the perceiver's task is to form an integrated final impression from the diverse attributes of the stimulus person. Thus it is not surprising that a traditional problem in the area has been the way in which these elements are combined. Does the order in which the perceiver considers various elements affect his final impression? Are some attributes of the stimulus person more important than others in organizing the resulting percept? In short, how does the way in which the stimulus is described affect the perceiver's impression?

Suppose that I described to you a hypothetical stimulus person and asked you to write a brief description of that person. If I tell you that the person is intelligent, industrious, impulsive, critical, stubborn, and envious, how happy and sociable will you believe that person to be? What if I gave you the same list of descriptive adjectives in the reverse order? Would simply changing the order shift your final impression? In one of the early laboratory studies of impression formation, Asch (1946) tried to answer just such questions. His subjects were instructed to form an integrated impression of a stimulus person from limited information he provided (the adjectives listed above). Half of the subjects received the adjectives in the order shown, while half received the reverse order. Asch found that subjects receiving the order beginning with "intelligent" were more likely to see the stimulus person as happy, humorous, sociable, and restrained than were subjects whose order began with "envious."

This apparently greater influence of early information was called the *primacy effect,* and Asch explained it in terms of word meaning. You will notice that the adjective list contains words that differ widely in desirability—while it is good to be intelligent, it is bad to be envious and stubborn. Asch argued that the early words in the series established an evaluative direction and that later adjectives were considered in light of this evaluation. In other words, the connotative meaning of "critical" may be different when interpreted as an attribute of an intelligent person than when seen as an attribute of an envious person. It is almost as though the perceiver makes a snap judgment on the basis of the first word in the series and then integrates the remainder of the description into the impression established by that word.

An alternative to Asch's suggestion of meaning change in primacy is the possibility that early words are simply given more weight in the impression. Suppose, for example, that you are given the same list of adjectives but are asked to refrain from forming a final impression until you have heard them all. This procedure should equalize the weight given to each adjective but should not affect any shifts in meaning. Thus, if the order makes a difference using this procedure, we would be more confident that meaning change had occurred. Using the same list of adjectives, Luchins (1957) performed this experiment and found that the primacy effect disappeared. In a similar approach to the problem, Anderson and Hubert (1963) used the same list but asked subjects to recall all of the adjectives before making their judgments. Their results also showed dissipation of the primacy effect in the recall condition. On the basis of this and other research, Anderson (1965) proposed an *information integration model* of impression formation to account for primacy. The model contends that the final impression is a weighted average of the incoming information and proposes a mathematical formula which specifies, among other things, the relative contributions of elements as a function of their position. The model has received support in a number of studies (Anderson, 1968, 1974; Himmelfarb and Senn, 1969; Oden and Anderson, 1971), and, as we shall see in Chapter 8, the general idea of a weighted average can also be used to describe the sequential process of dispositional attribution.

In the description of a social stimulus, then, the order of presentation of elements does seem to make a difference. What about the elements themselves? Again we begin with the classic study by Asch (1946). Just as Asch believed that primacy effects were attributable to meaning change in the later items, he thought that some adjectives might exert an organizing influence on those presented along with them. A person attempting to form an integrated impression from a list of traits might consider some of these more important or central than others. To test this idea, Asch presented a group of naive subjects with a list of traits: intelligent, skillful, industrious, warm, determined, practical, and cautious. Another group received the same list, except the word "cold" was substituted for "warm" in the series. All subjects were asked to write a brief paragraph describing the stimulus person and to indicate for a series of antonym pairs which antonym better described the person. The results showed that the warm-cold variable did make a substantial difference in the resulting impressions. The "warm" stimulus person was described as generous, humorous, happy, and humane, while the "cold" stimulus person was thought to be ungenerous, humorless, unhappy, and ruthless. It also appeared that the difference was not simply a matter of positive versus negative description, since both stimulus persons were described as curious, important, strong, and honest—all positive characteristics.

In an important extension of this study, Kelley (1950) showed that the warm-cold variable could influence behavior toward a live stimulus person as well as a hypothetical one. Students in three sections of a psychology course were told that there would be a guest instructor for an upcoming session, and then were given a brief, written biographical note about the guest. In fact there were two different biographical notes, one describing the guest instructor as "a rather warm person," the other stating that he was "a rather cold person," and both then describing him as "industrious, critical, practical, and determined." After a brief introduction, the guest instructor then led class discussion for a period of 20 minutes. During this time the experimenter recorded which students initiated discussion. After the 20 minutes had elapsed, all of the students were asked to rate the guest instructor on a series of adjective rating scales. Scores on these scales replicated the warm-cold perceptual differences found by Asch, and, more importantly, the behavioral results showed that students who were told that the instructor was warm initiated more discussion. While neither this study nor Asch's research directly answers the question of word meaning *change* (results from both could simply be the warm-cold difference, rather than any changes those words make in the other descriptive adjectives), both studies suggest that central traits can be important in impression formation and attribution.

The Total Self-presentation

Until now we have been speaking of the stimulus in person perception as it might be verbally described by a third party. The prerequisite for both order effects (primacy and recency) and combinatorial effects (central traits, weighted averaging) is a list of descriptive adjectives. Although such lists form the core of traditional impression-formation experiments (and generalize fairly well to attributions made from third-party descriptions), they are much less prevalent in first-hand observation. Only a well-schooled Boy Scout is likely to rattle off a series of descriptive adjectives—kind, cheerful, reverent, brave, and so forth—if asked for a self-description. Most people will start with a single trait or trait cluster and elaborate on it before moving on to others. In fact, studies with the Twenty Statements Test (Gordon, 1968; Kuhn and McPartland, 1954), in which the subject is asked to make 20 descriptive statements about himself in a period of 12 minutes, show that initial responses are primarily social categories—name, sex, race, religion, age—rather than descriptive adjectives.

In first-hand observation, the stimulus person's action and gestures will be almost as important as what he says, and your immediate presence will lead him to engage in what Goffman (1959) calls *self-presentation*. In Goffman's view, an encounter between two or more people involves a mutually agreed-upon set of rules that prescribe what behaviors are appropriate for the situation. Of course, there are different expectations for different circumstances—you don't behave in the same way around your parents that you do around your close friends—but in all cases some rules apply. Each person brings to the encounter what Goffman calls a *line*, a complete pattern of verbal and nonverbal acts through which he expresses his view of the situation and the participants (especially himself). This line can differ from situation to situation as the participants change, so it is best regarded as a subset of the stimulus person's total repertoire.

A central element of the person's line is his *face*, defined as the positive social value that the person claims for himself in the encounter. If all the information contributed by participants in the interaction is consistent with his positive social value, then the person is said to be "in face." In contrast, if some of the information provided by either self or others disconfirms the person's self-worth, then he is said to be "out of face." One of the most important rules of interaction is based on the *mutual commitment* involved in such encounters: Each participant's face becomes a property of the group, and all participants do what they can (within reason) to maintain each other's face. If you don't believe this, just try telling someone straight out, with no euphemisms, why you think he is perhaps the most obnoxious person you have ever met. Perhaps one of the most upsetting features of the student radicals of the sixties, at least as far as many older people were concerned, was their tendency to describe policies they disapproved of not with sophisticated derogatory terms but with profanity. They were somehow not playing the game properly, not letting other participants "save face."

The maintenance of face is not the goal of interaction, but rather is a necessary condition for its continuation. When you are conversing with close friends, your primary goal is not self-aggrandizement but the conduct of a relationship in which all of you can express your true feelings, exchange ideas, and only occasionally pat each other on the back. If any "incidents" occur that threaten the face of a participant, however, a corrective process called *face-work* will be initiated to preserve the interaction. Four fundamental stages seem to be involved in this process. First, there is a *challenge* to the threatening incident. One of your friends has just made a suggestion, and you have blurted out, "Hey, that's really a dumb idea." This is correctly perceived by the others as a threat to your friend's face, and their disapproving looks challenge that threat. In the second stage of the corrective process you have a chance to redefine the incident and so remove its threatening import. You make an *offering*, such as "Aw, I was only joking." If your offering is satisfactory, the offended person then *accepts* it and finally you convey your *thanks* to the others for permitting you to correct the situation.

There can, of course, be significant departures from this basic ritual order. You can initiate an offering before a challenge has been issued, or the threatened person can make excuses for your behavior. You can continue the offering beyond an initial acceptance to make sure that his feelings aren't hurt. Or, as is more frequent in adversary relationships, the offender can refuse to make an offering. Should there be such a refusal, the offended parties can make an aggressive response designed to destroy your face, or they can withdraw self-righteously, confident that someone else will show you the error of your ways.

Goffman's ritual analysis of interaction serves to illustrate two aspects of the crucial difference between a stimulus object and a stimulus person: (1) properties are selected by the person for presentation, and (2) observation is a social behavior. First, when the stimulus for perception is an object, even an animate though infrahuman one, nearly all of its properties are accessible to the perceiver. Although mediating conditions may preclude full knowledge (it is difficult to tell the color of an object in the dark), those conditions are not under the active control of the object itself. In contrast, when the stimulus is a person there is an active selection of *which* verbal and nonverbal behaviors to reveal, and that choice depends on the situation. Second, person perception is an interpersonal phenomenon, governed by the same kinds of rules and expectations that regulate other forms of social interaction. What behaviors the stimulus person chooses to emit can have implications for the perceiver, and the impressions the perceiver forms can in the same way affect the stimulus person. The social nature of person perception thus places restrictions and expectations upon both participants.

We began this chapter with some conceptual similarities between object perception and person perception, and we ended with the crucial differences. In the formal lens model of perception it mattered little whether the distal stimulus was a person or an object; the final percept arising from that distal stimulus was produced in much the same manner. The categorization model of perception began to consider some of the ways that a stimulus person might differ from a stimulus object, qualitatively as well as quantitatively, and these differences were carried over into a discussion of the stimulus description. Finally, we took into account the stimulus person's participation in generating an impression. A stimulus person is not merely a collection of unrelated perceptual cues. He is a thinking and volitional being actively involved in self-presentation.

3

THE ELEMENTS OF ATTRIBUTION

Reread

We have briefly considered some of the phenomena of person perception, and we have seen how the effective stimulus consists of the *not so* complete pattern of verbal and nonverbal behaviors presented more *consciously* or less consciously by the stimulus person. Now as we begin to focus our attention on the more narrowly bounded body of attribution theory, we turn to the contribution of the perceiver. Anyone who has listened to the court testimony of several eyewitnesses to a crime knows that different perceivers can form quite divergent impressions from exactly the same stimulus material. The same is true for more routine attributions. Whether the perceiver's role is described as performing the constructive process, as engaging in categorization, or as making dispositional attributions, it is an *active* role that contributes meaning to the perceptual result. To clarify the perceiver's place in the process, we first consider some of the factors that can contribute to accuracy in interpersonal judgment and then identify some of the motivational influences that can lead to perceptual and attributional distortion. The chapter concludes with an outline of the basic stages of the attribution process.

Why Are Perceivers as Accurate as They Are?

Consider, for example, the confidence man. Whether he is touting the curative powers of a secret elixir, offering partnerships in enticing business ventures, or selling homesites in the middle of the ocean, his livelihood (not to mention his freedom) depends on accuracy in interpersonal judgment. Even though there may well be "a sucker born every minute," the confidence man's task is not an easy one. He must identify likely prospects for his wares, establish his credibility and make the sale, and then "cool the mark out" (Goffman, 1952) to preclude later prosecution. The penalty for mistakes is high—a single rube who notifies the authorities can spell the end of his promising career. That successful wheeler-dealers are most staunchly defended by the very people they victimize suggests not only how convincing they were, but also how carefully their prospects were chosen. What sorts of factors contribute to such accuracy in interpersonal judgment?

Intuitively, we might identify several possibilities. First, an accurate judge might have a great deal of *experience* with the target population. Not only should he have a similar cultural background, he should be familiar with local idioms and customs in order to understand all the information available to him. He should know from this experience where the individuals' expertise lies (in order to avoid issues that they understand well) and what their weaknesses are (in order to exploit them). He should know what their motivations are and how they will respond to various sorts of appeals. Second, since the accurate assessment of other people is a cognitive process, we might expect that more *intelligent* people would make better judges. Interpersonal judgment is to no small degree an information-processing task. The con man must discern relevant information from all that he knows about the target person, must keep in mind his prior experience with similar others, and must individualize his pitch to take advantage of the target person's unique frailties. It stands to reason that these abilities should be related to more general intellectual capability. Finally, our con man should have the ability to put himself in the target person's shoes. He should be skilled at what Mead (1934) called "taking the role of the other," and since his pitch is often laden with emotion, he should have *empathy* with the target person's emotional state. These three criteria —experience, intelligence, and empathic ability—ought to increase the accuracy of interpersonal judgments made by any perceivers, not just by confidence men.

Unfortunately, even though there has long been an interest in the "ability to judge others," the present state of research in the area adds little to our intuitive notions. A number of studies (reviewed by Cline, 1964) suggest the importance of *similarity* between the judge and the target person but provide little evidence for a general judging ability. (Cronbach [1955] provides an important critique of early judgmental accuracy research.) In addition, some recent experimental studies of empathy (narrowly defined in these studies as experiencing the same emotions felt by a stimulus person) have also found differences based on similarity (Stotland, Sherman, and Shaver, 1971). Finally, Allport (1961) has concluded that intelligence, good personal adjustment, and aesthetic ability all contribute to judging ability.

It is probably fair to say that perceivers are as accurate as they are because of substantial shared experience, because of the amount of information available (at a minimum, several discrete bits of information all indicating the presence of a single trait), and because the inferences to be made are usually rather straightforward. Individual differences in perceivers' ability to make such interpersonal judgments accurately are probably related to differences in experience, intelligence, and empathic ability.

How Can Motivation Affect the Perceiver's Judgments?

The almost universal presence of referees in organized sports activities testifies to the fact that people who have a stake in the outcome of ambiguous perceptual decisions have difficulty remaining objective. Blind grading of examinations, elaborate controls for experimenter bias in social research, and dismissals of potential jurors "for cause" are other evidence of the difficulty of maintaining objectivity in interpersonal judgments. How do a perceiver's personality characteristics, experience, and personal motives produce errors in person perception and attribution?

Let us begin with relatively enduring personality dispositions. If two perceivers, one highly authoritarian and one egalitarian, are asked to describe the hue, brightness, and saturation of each of a set of colored discs, their descriptions are apt to be quite similar. If the task is extended to include their feelings about, and their emotional reactions to, these colored discs, the descriptions will begin to diverge. Indeed, the recently popular Lüscher Color Test (Lüscher, 1969), which attempts to differentiate among personality types on the basis of emotional reactions to colors, relies almost exclusively upon such divergence. Finally, changing the object of perception from an inanimate stimulus to a person will produce even greater differences. From what is known of the "authoritarian personality" (Adorno et al., 1951; Christie, 1954), the authoritarian's description of a stimulus person is likely to be laden with terms relating to power, toughness, and self-control. The egalitarian's description will probably concentrate more on the stimulus person's human characteristics. In the broadest sense, the stimulus situation will *mean* different things to perceivers who differ.

The most comprehensive examination of the effects of enduring personality differences upon social perception is the work of George Kelly (1955, 1963). Like Bruner (1957) and Heider (1958), Kelly views man as a perceptual problem solver: the perceiver approaches each social situation with an expectation or hypothesis about it and then compares this hypothesis to the reality of the situation. Kelly calls the perceiver's hypotheses *personal constructs*, and he shows how they are interrelated into a consistent scheme. Although perceivers can have similar sets of personal constructs, no two sets are ever exactly alike.

Since the personal constructs that a perceiver holds determine the way in which he views the world, Kelly thought it essential to develop a method for measuring the constructs used. This method is the Role Construct Repertory (or "Rep") Test, which asks subjects to compare the occupants of various role positions (such as boss, subordinate, parent, person you dislike, friend, spouse). The roles are presented in triads, and you are asked to tell how two members of each triad are like each other but different from the third. For example, how are "parent" and "boss" like each other but different from "friend"? Your answers to this test yield a number of interesting elements: which constructs you choose (such as likability, equality, power), how many different constructs you have employed, and the relative frequency of each one used. One of the more fruitful individual differences identified through variants of the "Rep" test is the dimension of *cognitive complexity*. While this dimension is usually defined simply in terms of the total number of constructs used, it has been shown to be related to various aspects of social perception, from ability to form an integrated impression of a stimulus person when given conflicting descriptive information (Bieri, 1961) to susceptibility to social influence (McGuire, 1968).

Individual differences in cognitive complexity and stable personality traits produce relatively enduring differences between perceivers, but more transient motivational factors can also affect person perception. This interaction between motivation and perception is not a novel idea in psychology. The insertion of "catch trials"—trials where no stimulus is presented, but the subject is still supposed to respond—in classic psychophysical studies was a hedge against the overly cooperative subject who would otherwise hesitate to say that he perceived nothing. From a completely different perspective, the psychoanalytic concept of *projection* of one's own negative qualities outward onto other people also assumes an interaction between motivation and perception.

While a large number of studies have been done—often from quite different theoretical bases—that can be used to illustrate motivational effects on social perception, perhaps the most well known are the series of experiments that in the 1940s constituted a "New Look" in perception. In a comprehensive review, Allport (1955) grouped these experiments into six broad categories according to the presumed source of motivational influence. They indicate that (1) bodily needs such as hunger (Levine, Chein, and Murphy, 1942), (2) simple reward and punishment (Schaefer and Murphy, 1943), (3) the monetary value of the object (Bruner and Goodman, 1947), (4) the perceiver's system of personal values (Postman, Bruner, and McGinnies, 1948), (5) personality characteristics (Catell and Wenig, 1952), and (6) perceptual defense (McGinnies, 1949) participate in the process of perception. Because of its self-protective nature, and because of its impact on later research, perceptual defense deserves some further comment.

According to Allport (1955, p. 321), perceptual defense presented the most formidable theoretical difficulties at the same time that it was "the winner of all honors for revolutionary outlook. . . . We have for some time been accustomed to psychoanalytic mechanisms of repression, wish-fullfillment, and rationalization as influences that distort the way we *believe, feel,* or *think.* When, however, this 'functionalistic' idea is extended to the perceptions of normal college students looking at words in a tachistoscope, we have something new."

Let us suppose that you are a subject in this revolutionary experiment. You arrive at the experimental laboratory and after listening to some introductory remarks by the experimenter are seated in front of a tachistoscope, a device for presenting visual stimuli with precise controls for illumination and duration of display. You are told that a series of stimulus words will be presented on the screen, one at a time. The first time that each word is presented, it will be shown for so short a time that you will not be able to tell what it is. Gradually the presentation duration will be increased until you can correctly report to the experimenter what the word is. The time required for correct perception will be your score for that word. Ready?

What the subjects were not told was that some of the words in the list were neutral ones such as apple, child, and danced, while the remaining words were *critical* ones such as bitch, whore, and raped. By today's standards these certainly do not seem like "critical" words that subjects would hesitate to report, but that was a different time. At any rate, McGinnies (1949) found that greater exposure times were required for recognition of the critical words, that the prerecognition guesses of those words were nonsense while the guesses of the neutral words were structurally similar to the real word, and that a physiological measure of arousal during prerecognition showed greater arousal when a critical word was being displayed. From these results he concluded that the critical words were threatening, and that to defend against that threat the perceivers tried not to perceive them—hence the name *perceptual defense*.

As critics of the concept were quick to point out (e.g., Hochberg and Gleitman, 1950), perceptual defense has a peculiar quality: there must be a little censor in your head that perceives things before you do and then screens out the things that are threatening. Particularly in view of some of the methodological problems in McGinnies's experiment, such as lack of control for frequency of occurrence in natural language (Howes and Solomon, 1950), the preperception screening explanation was generally unconvincing. Much more plausible was the suggestion that there was delay not in perceiving the critical words, but rather in reporting them to the experimenter. When the report is apt to be embarrassing, you simply want to be sure before you commit yourself. Although there is still some disagreement over the precise mechanisms involved, the idea that motivation can influence perception is well accepted today (e.g., see the review by Eriksen and Eriksen, 1972). Particularly as the stimulus situation becomes more ambiguous, and as the perceiver's motivation increases, perception and attribution are increasingly affected by motivational factors.

The research summarized here suggests that while in the large majority of cases people make fairly accurate judgments about each other, there will be important instances in which perceivers will arrive at biased attributions. In order to understand just how these errors can arise, we need to specify in greater detail the nature of the attribution process. Models of the process have been proposed by Heider (1958), Jones and Davis (1965), and Kelley (1967), and these will be discussed in Chapter 4. Before turning to the formal models, it will be helpful to consider the basic stages of attribution in terms of their temporal order. Not only can this provide a framework for the later presentation of the three models, it can be helpful in the comparisons between models to be made in Chapter 5.

Stages of the Attribution Process

THE BEGINNING: OBSERVATION OF AN ACTION

As a necessary first step in the attribution process, there must be the observation of an action. In the case of self-perception (discussed more fully in Chapter 6), only the actor would need to be present, although other people could be, and often are, involved. Both in the development of certain skills and in the change of interpersonal behaviors, it can be quite helpful to "see ourselves as others see us." For years most college and professional football teams have used game films to identify and correct mistakes that individuals, or the team as a whole, might have made in the course of a game. A person taking golf lessons from a professional might be shown a slow-motion film of his swing in order to correct a persistent slice. One of the major objectives of the encounter group movement has been to provide participants with feedback about their social stimulus value to others.

In all of these cases some external means is used to help the actor regard himself as an object. This distinction between the actor as a behaving person and as an object of his own reflective assessment of that behavior was first proposed by William James (1892) and has played an important role in the subsequent development of self-concept theory (Cooley, 1902; Duval and Wicklund, 1972; Gordon and Gergen, 1968; Mead, 1934). For our present purposes it is sufficient to be aware that a single person can be both actor and observer of his own action, and that self-observation of some form is a prerequisite for self-attribution.

When the stimulus is another person, the perceiver may observe that actor in person, may view a representation such as film or videotape of the action, or may be informed in some less direct manner (in writing, through the account of a first-hand observer, through hearsay) that the behavior in question has taken place. We shall see that as the perceiver becomes farther removed from the action, and as he relies more heavily on information provided by intermediaries (who may or may not be reliable), the potential for misinterpretation becomes much greater. In any event, the action, including the behavior of choosing not to act, must still be observed and related to the perceiver if it is to be the basis for a later attribution.

THE MIDDLE: JUDGMENT OF INTENTION

But is all observed behavior attributionally meaningful? Probably not. Generally speaking, to be attributionally useful an observed action must be judged to have been the product of an intention. For example, involuntary actions usually reveal little about the underlying dispositions of an actor, although in some instances the manner in which these actions are performed can provide clues to the actor's emotional state. The fact that a person is breathing is attributionally uninformative (apart from indicating that he is alive), but rapid and shallow breathing can suggest the presence of an emotional state of fear. Certainly this is information about the actor, but our interest as perceivers is not so much in the actor's temporary emotional state as in the possible reasons for that state, and these must be inferred from the situational context.

In a similar manner, the routine performance of a habit—in and of itself—attests only to the existence of the habit. My observation of a person lighting a cigarette reveals to me only that this is a person who smokes cigarettes, not why he chose to light up at this particular time. Some habits may, by their existence, reveal dispositions (a classic Freudian psychoanlayst might well attribute smoking to some deep-seated oral fixation), and the context in which the action occurs (the person lights a cigarette as he enters his boss's office to ask for a raise) may provide the opportunity for a dispositional attribution, but a single isolated occurrence of habitual action is usually attributionally valueless.

In contrast to involuntary, routine, or habitual actions are those that appear to be the *product of intention*. To many philosophers, and not a few psychologists, description of behavior as "intentional" would seem a battle cry for free will. The argument goes this way: It makes sense to describe behavior as intentional only if man has the capacity to exercise free will in making choices among the range of behaviors possible in any particular situation. Without that capacity, all behavior is seen as determined not by individual beings but by environmental (or even cosmic) forces beyond individual control. While the determinism–free will controversy is surely an important one, it is not our purpose here to add fuel to the fire. Attribution theorists, as observers of human behavior, recognize that not only do people often behave as if they believed in free will, people have institutionalized the concept of intentionality in their systems of law. Precisely because they are psychologists, rather than philosophers, attribution theorists can agree that only intentionally produced actions (as we have used the term above) should be attributionally meaningful, and then disagree about whether the dispositions giving rise to these intentions are personal or environmental, without directly confronting the issue of determinism versus free will.

Thus, from the psychologist's point of view, to be attributionally valuable an action must be judged to have originated from an intention. But how is it possible for a perceiver to guess which of several alternative intentions actually led to the observed behavior? To this question philosophers such as Anscombe (1957, p. 8) reply that "if you want to say at least some true things about a man's intentions, you will have a strong chance of success if you mention what he actually did, or is doing." That there will be a strong chance of success leaves open the potential for failure: an observer's description may not always coincide with either the actor's own description or the description that might be made by other observers. There are several reasons that discrepancies in description might arise, even assuming the truthfulness of all concerned. First, an action can have many different descriptions. "Driving an automobile" can simultaneously be described by the driver as "beginning a vacation," by a policeman as "exceeding the speed limit," and by an environmentalist as "polluting the air." Second, an action can have consequences apparent to an observer that would be unnoticed by the actor. For example, a skier making his way across an Alpine snowfield would most probably not describe his behavior as "starting an avalanche," although an observer below, who could see the beginnings of fault lines behind the skier, might well give such a description. Another possibility is the existence of some psychodynamic influence, in either the actor or the observer, that would contribute to an unconscious distortion of the description of the action. Ultimately, the careful perceiver will rely on his assessment of the circumstances surrounding the action, on his other knowledge of the actor, and on his own past experience as an actor in similar situations to arrive at a choice of an intention behind the action.

The End: Making a Dispositional Attribution

Although it is intuitively plausible that the attribution process should begin with the observation of an action and should involve a judgment of intention, it is less obvious that the end of the inferential chain should be a *dispositional attribution.* Two important alternatives need to be considered in light of the joint goals of inference —explanation and prediction—discussed in Chapter 1. First, is dispositional attribution unnecessary because the identification of the intention behind an action provides an adequate explanation by itself? And second, is dispositional attribution too little, because it fails to give sufficient weight to the environment as an ultimate cause of behavior?

Why is judgment of intention alone not a satisfactory end of the inference process? As illustrated in Chapter 1, the perceiver's motivation to engage in attribution is a need to simplify his perceptual world by *explaining* the present and past behavior of others and by *predicting* with some degree of accuracy what those people are likely to do in the future. Now, in comparison to identification of the intention, a *dispositional attribution* is superior on both of these counts. It provides an answer to the question "Why?" that is a more fully satisfactory explanation, and at the same time is a better estimate of future action.

Suppose, for example, that a swinging bachelor friend of mine has, for his first date with a highly attractive young woman, splurged on a lavish evening beginning with dinner at an exclusive French restaurant, followed by a concert, and concluding with drinks at an after-hours nightspot. As he returns her to her apartment, she initiates a most fond farewell. It is clear that her actions are intentional and that the immediate purpose of her intention is to give pleasure to them both. Nevertheless, my friend may well wonder whether the source of the intention is *environmental*—a product of the situation, likely to be repeated only under similar circumstances in the future —or a *personal disposition* of liking for him—implying that she would behave toward him in the same manner under entirely different future conditions. We might guess that my friend would be biased toward the latter interpretation, but the essential point is that *whatever* the interpretation is, it adds to our understanding of the action and to our subjective estimate of our ability to predict the occurrence of such actions in the future. Thus, attribution of an intention to a dispositional source either in the environment or in the actor will help us to achieve the joint inference goals of explanation and prediction.

But is such a dispositional attribution necessarily the final link in the inference chain? For most of us, attribution of an intention to an environmental disposition does end the chain of inference. In the case of a dispositional attribution to a person, however, the picture is somewhat more cloudy. Just as the dispositional attribution provides the source of intention, which is the source of the action, it could be argued that factors in the person's past experience or present environment are the source of his personal disposition. Indeed, this is exactly the kind of argument that often distinguishes between political liberals and political conservatives in discussions of social problems. The conservative is apt, for example, to attribute unemployment to the fact that "people on the welfare rolls simply do not want to work" (attribution terminating in a personal disposition). While agreeing that this assertion may be true, a liberal might well say, "Of course they don't want to work. They have been so culturally deprived and so poorly educated that they have never had any success in work situations, and until we can find ways to give them sufficient self-confidence to try again, they will remain on the welfare rolls." It is important to emphasize that this is not a disagreement regarding the existence of personal dispositions—both the liberal and the conservative agree that the immediate source of intentions to not work is a personal disposition against participation in the economic system. The only difference is that the conservative's inference chain ends with the personal disposition, while the liberal's goes a step farther to ask about the environmental source of that personal disposition.

How are we to determine which of these end points is more appropriate for the ideal attribution process as we have been discussing it? Recall the two objectives of attribution, explanation and prediction. In each of the preceding steps in the attribution process, there has been an increment in both our understanding of the action and our ability to predict its future occurrence. We cannot understand or predict an action we do not observe; identification of an intention behind an observed action serves to increase both understanding and predictive ability; attribution of that intention to a disposition (either environmental or personal) also contributes to both explanation and prediction. In contrast, going beyond a personal disposition to its presumed source may enhance our understanding, but it will not materially affect our ability to predict what a particular actor is apt to do in the future. When the dispositional attribution has been to the environment, even those who believe that the environment is as it is because of some supernatural influence will not argue that this knowledge increases their predictive ability. When the dispositional attribution has been a personal one, the same argument is valid: if a man has a disposition to avoid participation in the economic system, there is no increase in predictive ability gained by asserting that the source of this disposition is the individual's past experience. Since any environmental changes would be reflected in a changed disposition before being seen in changed intentions, identification of the source of a disposition does not increase predictive ability beyond a level already reached through knowledge of the disposition. Since we have argued that the goals of the attribution process are *both* explanation and prediction, it is reasonable to identify as the end of the process that point at which there is a final increment in both.

THE CHAIN OF INFERENCE

The process of attribution may require only fractions of a second to complete—a "snap judgment"—or it may, as in the case of jury deliberations of dispositional guilt or innocence, take a period of weeks. A final example shows how the process can be conceptualized as a flow chart (Fig. 3-1) regardless of its length in real time. At each stage in the chain of inference there are several possibilities, and only a single path will ultimately lead to an attribution to a personal disposition of the actor.

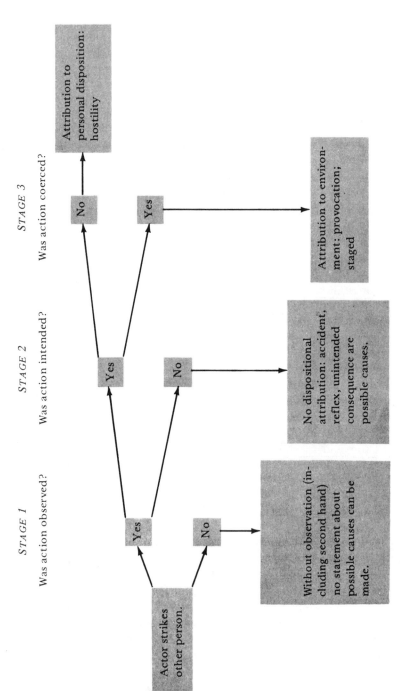

Figure 3-1. Flowchart for attribution of an action to a personal disposition of the actor.

While out for a walk in his favorite city park, our ideal attributor comes across two men talking to each other. They continue talking in an animated way as the perceiver approaches, but as he gets very close one of the men suddenly strikes the other, knocking him to the ground, and walks away. The perceiver has observed an action (Stage 1 in the diagram). What is he likely to consider as he attempts to make an attribution to account for the action?

Having observed the action, the perceiver will then wonder whether it was intentionally produced, as shown in Stage 2. From the manner in which the blow was delivered, the impersonal alternatives—involuntary reflex, accident, and unintended consequence of some other intentional action—will most probably be ruled out. It should be emphasized that designating these as "impersonal" alternatives is not meant to imply that they were somehow not connected with the actor, but rather that they are alternatives that would not lead to a personal *dispositional* attribution. Thus, in Stage 2 a decision will probably be made that the actor intended to strike the other person.

Having established to his satisfaction *what* has happened, our perceiver will now begin to wonder *why* the action might have occurred. Again, as Stage 3 of the diagram indicates, there are two basic possibilities: attribution is made either to personal disposition or to environmental influence. First among the environmental alternatives is legitimate provocation. The gestures accompanying the conversation could have been misinterpreted by the attacker as threatening, although they did not appear to be so to the perceiver. Even in the absence of physical threat, a verbal provocation could have been issued by the one who was struck, but his apparent surprise at the blow argues against this interpretation. In addition, there is a second category of possible environmental reasons: the entire scenario could have been staged just for the perceiver's benefit. People sometimes play practical jokes of this kind on unsuspecting passers-by, criminals can use diversions to prevent onlookers from noticing something more important nearby, and recently even social psychologists have begun staging such situations to assess bystander intervention in emergencies. However, the proportion of staged events to real events is still quite low, and so, more by elimination than by assertion, our perceiver may arrive at an attribution of personal disposition to the actor. The only remaining possibility is that the actor is a hostile and dangerous person.

Attribution theory attempts to specify processes within the perceiver that are involved in his explanation and prediction of the behavior of others. These interpersonal judgments are often accurate but can sometimes be influenced by the perceiver's motivation. At each stage along the chain to a personal attribution, the perceiver adds both to his understanding of the reasons for the action and to his ability to predict its future occurrence. An action that is not observed cannot be understood or predicted to recur; intended actions are more stable and meaningful than are accidents or reflexes; and personal dispositions are thought to be more easily and completely categorized than are situations. While it would be possible for the perceiver to wonder about the source of an actor's disposition—"Is he a product of a broken home?" or "Is he an incorrigible reject of society?"—and while the answers to these questions might increase the perceiver's understanding, there would be no improvement in the perceiver's ability to predict whether the actor would repeat his performance in the future. For this reason, the attribution process is considered to terminate in the dispositional attribution.—

Not necessarily so!

4

THREE ATTRIBUTION
THEORIES

In preceding chapters it has been shown that perceivers engage in
an active search for the meaning of, and reasons for, the behavior of
other persons. The elements of this attribution process include, at
the very least, observation of the action (first hand or through vari- *l.*
ous possible intermediaries), a judgment by the perceiver that the *2*
action was the product of an intention, and the final inference of an *3.*
underlying disposition to account for the presence of that intention.
This chapter presents the three principal theories that have been
proposed to explain how that attribution process might occur and to
specify some of the factors that might be involved.

Heider's Naive Psychology of Attribution

The comprehensive and fruitful work of Fritz Heider is a formaliza-
tion of the ways in which any layman might try to understand the
behavior of an actor. Not everyone has access to the principles of
scientific psychology and its explanations of human behavior, yet we
all do attribute responsibility for actions and events, talk of the enduring personality characteristics of other people, and assess the
relative contributions of skill, motivation, and luck to task outcomes.
What questions do we, as *naive psychologists* (ordinary people trying
to understand behavior), ask in order to make these attributions?
What characteristics of the situation, of the actor, or of ourselves as
perceivers lead us to choose one attribution over another? How does
the "man on the street" come to *know* the causes of action?

These questions deal with the phenomenal (perceptual) experience of the perceiver, and Heider's answers reflect his training in

the Gestalt tradition of psychology. The Gestaltists emphasized the importance of describing the perceiver's subjective experience rather than concentrating exclusively on objective description of the stimulus input. With perceptual demonstrations such as the *phi phenomenon,* in which two alternately blinking lights can give rise to the subjective experience of movement, the Gestaltists illustrated that the perceptual product is often quite different from what would be expected simply on the basis of an objective description of the physical stimulus. And the conclusion drawn from these illustrations is that not only is the subjective experience of the perceiver a legitimate object of study, it may be essential for complete understanding of how the perceiver views his world.

In the case of social perception, especially when the stimulus is an action, even a detailed physical description may not be satisfactory. For example, imagine that we are omniscient observers watching an encounter between you and one of your professors. In this case the professor is the *actor,* and is telling you (the *perceiver*), "I thought that you made some excellent contributions to the class discussion today." An objective description of this behavior might include a detailed analysis of the grammatical structure of the comment, a summary of its semantic content, and a listing of the actor's characteristics, including his relationship to you. But is this sufficient? Won't you as a perceiver also want to know what the stimulus in its context means to you? Does the professor think your performance was good because everyone else was behaving stupidly, or were you just that much better than others who were also doing well? Perhaps more importantly, does this one item of behavior represent an underlying *disposition:* was it simply a pleasant comment, or will it be reflected in your grade? Heider's theory holds that the function of social perception is to enable perceivers to discover these underlying regularities—dispositions—that would make the perceiver's world a more predictable, and hence a more controllable, place.

THE PROBLEM OF PHENOMENAL CAUSALITY

Although Heider's adaptation of the lens model of perception (discussed in Chapter 2) specifies processes that might be involved in the observation of an action, most of his theoretical work dealt with the other two essentials of attribution—judgments of intention and the making of dispositional attributions. Heider's interest in the first of these processes began with his studies of how perceivers make judgments of causality in situations in which persons are *not* involved. Just as the stimulus conditions of the phi phenomenon give rise to a perceptual experience of movement, there should be stimulus conditions that produce a phenomenal experience of causality.

In an early investigation of the phenomenal perception of "apparent" behavior, Heider and Simmel (1944) showed subjects a brief film depicting the interrelated movements of two triangles and a circle in the vicinity of a large rectangle, a section of which could be opened and closed. The arrangement of these shapes is shown in Figure 4-1. During the course of the film, the shapes moved about as follows: The larger triangle (*T*) entered the "house" and then emerged to "fight" with the smaller triangle (*t*). During the battle the circle (*c*) moved inside the house. After winning the fight, *T* moved into the house and pursued *c* around the interior. Then *t* opened the "door," *c* moved out, followed by *T*, and the three moved around the outside of the house twice. Finally, *t* and *c* left the field, and *T* battered the walls of the house until they broke into pieces. The film was shown to three groups of female subjects: to one with a very general instruction to interpret the film, and to a second with the instruction to interpret the movements as the actions of persons. For the third group the instructions were similar to those of the second group, but the film was shown in reverse. Not only did almost all of the subjects (111 out of 114 across conditions) interpret the movements as the actions of animated beings, primarily humans, but in the two forward conditions rather uniform motives were attributed as the causes of these actions.

Although this paper is of some importance for the part it played in stimulating Heider's ideas about attribution, its results considered alone are equivocal. Not only were the procedure and instructions greatly loaded in favor of the attribution of personal causality and motivation (see Orne, 1962) but, as Heider himself stated in the

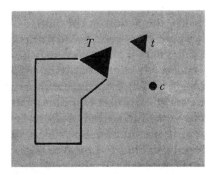

Figure 4-1. Geometrical figures used in the study of phenomenal causality. (Adapted from Heider and Simmel, 1944.)

Method section of the paper), "In the . . . description of the main features of the picture, the action is, for purposes of reference, divided into scenes. A few 'anthropomorphic' words are used since a description in purely geometrical terms would be too complicated and too difficult to understand." Analogously, there is no reason to suppose that the subjects reported anything other than the simplest description—an anthropomorphic one. For example, a subject describing the movements might say things like "T came out and started fighting with t," "T chased c around inside the house," and "T chased t and c around outside the house." When the experimenter asked this subject, "What kind of person is T?" the subject would have considered his own descriptions of the action—and the fact that T is *larger* than t—and would have replied with the typical answer obtained, "T is a bully."

Persons as the Prototype of Origins

The spirit of this empirical study was represented in the first theoretical paper by the idea that persons are the "prototype of origins." In other words, saying that the action of a person is the origin of an event is the simplest and most satisfying explanation for the event's occurrence. Indeed, the actor's behavior is so overwhelming that it "engulfs the field," often obscuring truly environmental causes. Some recent research, to be discussed in Chapters 6 and 8, suggests how the tendency of behavior to engulf the field can distort both self-attributions and attributions made to others.

There are several possible sources of the tendency to view persons as the prototype of origins. First, there is the *relative simplicity* of causality when another explanation would require more extensive cognitive work. The Heider and Simmel study is an excellent example of this factor at work. Not only would it have been more difficult for subjects to verbalize the action in the film, as Heider points out, but the movements would have been more difficult to understand. A second but related possibility is that there may be bias in the attributional processes of adults left over from their *cognitive organization* as young children. Piaget (1932) has illustrated how the child's early perception of the world confuses simultaneous occurrence with causality—if a child wishes for a desired object, and the object happens to appear at that moment quite by chance, the child will believe that his wish produced the object. This obviously exaggerated sense of personal causality is the basis for an attribution of similar capability to others. In the course of his subsequent development, the child learns that effects are not produced by wishes alone, but the bias toward personal causality may still persist.

A third source of the tendency to consider persons to be funda- *Correspon-*
mental origins is related to the *similarity* between the person and the *dent*
event. Especially on value-related dimensions—such as morality, *Inferences*
trustworthiness, and personal worth—the properties of an act may
be described by the same words that are used to refer to the person. ↓
Consider, for example, the statement "But he didn't look like a *Jones +*
criminal!" Evidently people carry with them an image of the physical *Davies*
appearance that a criminal should have. And, upon meeting an unfamiliar person whose honesty must be ascertained, this image is
brought to mind and compared with the appearance of the person.
An expectancy regarding honesty is generated by the comparison,
and the perceiver then behaves in accordance with this expectancy.
In addition to physical appearance, other dimensions of similarity,
such as the moral character of the person and action and the
perceiver's emotional reaction to both, may also affect attribution.

The perceiver's own *needs and attitudes* are a fourth source of the
bias toward overattribution of personal causality. Locating the causes
of one's failures in another person not only provides the reason for
past failures—as would attribution to impersonal sources—but also
serves as an excuse for those in the future, as an impersonal attribution would not. "Somebody is out to get me" implies that the somebody will continue his attacks indefinitely, while "My luck has been
very bad" does not carry the same implication and offers no
psychological protection against failures to come. In much the same
manner, locating the source of harm to oneself in another person
creates a ready outlet for aggression difficult to direct at an impersonal cause. A final example of the dynamic nature of attribution is
the ascribing of responsibility to persons as a means of maintaining
certain attitudes. An extremist politician will locate the responsibility
for change away from his views in the "agitations" of his enemies
instead of in the changing attitudes of the general society.

THE NAIVE ANALYSIS OF ACTION

In Heider's later work (1958), his emphasis was less upon the
factors that might produce overattribution to personal causality than
upon the rational process involved in distinguishing among varying
degrees of personal responsibility. He suggested that two general *internal*
classes of force, personal and environmental, enter into the produc- *external -*
tion of action, and he asserted that the amount of personal causality *Kelly*
attributed would vary with the estimated extent to which personal
force had determined the effect.

What are the components of personal and environmental force
that the perceiver might consider in making this determination? The

possibilities can be seen in the following example. Let us assume that we are watching a person paddle a canoe across a swiftly flowing river toward another person standing on the opposite bank. As the diagram (Fig. 4–2) shows, personal force is subdivided into two principal components, ability and trying. *Ability* refers to the physical or mental skill, power, or capacity required to perform the action. Our example illustrated that a person's ability can be affected by: (1) his *knowledge* of such things as how to use the paddle effectively to keep from going around in circles, the fact that he must paddle in the upstream direction to counteract the force of the river flow; (2) his *attitudes,* such as belief in his power to accomplish the task; (3) *variable personal factors,* such as fatigue or mood (it should be clear from the example that these variable factors may change not only between performances of different actions, but also during the course of a single lengthy performance); (4) *physical possessions* and position (have you ever tried to paddle a canoe with your hands?); (5) the *opinions* and suggestions of others; and (6) *personal needs* of a psychodynamic nature (we would expect a person with underlying

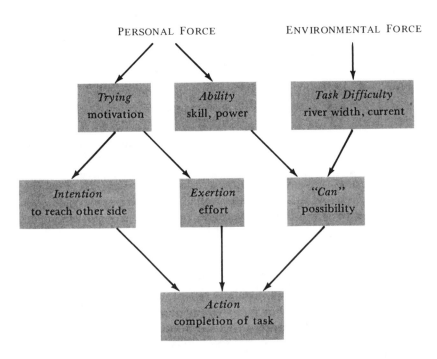

Figure 4-2. The personal and environmental components of action. (Adapted from Heider, 1958.)

self-hatred to be more likely than average to be swept down the river to the falls).

But the determination of whether our actor can successfully perform the intended action cannot be made from knowledge of his ability alone. His ability must be balanced against the environmental force that is in opposition to successful completion. Foremost among the components of environmental force is the stable dispositional property of *task difficulty*. How wide is the river? How swift is the current? Only if the actor's judged ability exceeds the task difficulty does the system attain what Heider refers to as the dispositional state of *can*. In addition to the stable property of task difficulty, there are variable factors in the environment that can change the balance between ability and difficulty. For example, *luck* can momentarily change the balance either in the actor's favor or against him: a fresh breeze blowing in the direction that he is going might increase his likelihood of success, while a thunderstorm with high winds blowing against him would most probably decrease his chances of crossing.

The conjunction of ability and task difficulty (with whatever variable environmental factors are present at the time) determines whether the action is possible. Completion of a possible action requires the second essential component of personal force—*trying*. Heider (1958, p. 100) defines trying as "the motivational factor that . . . propels and guides the action and gives it its purposive character." Personal causality is distinguished first by *intention* from cases in which the person is merely part of the sequence of events. Also excluded from the class of personal causality are cases in which the action in question is the unintended consequence of a different intentional act. This restriction of the class is not thought of as excluding unconscious intentions: "Often it is precisely because such action displays the features of personal causality . . . that inferences are drawn concerning unconscious motivations and unconscious goals" (pp. 100–101). The class of intention is further restricted to refer only to *what* a person is trying to accomplish, not why he is trying to accomplish it. This limitation is imposed to exclude intentions that are not directly linked with behavior, e.g., an intention to accomplish a certain end in the absence of knowledge of how to bring about that end. Personal desire—when connected to behavior—is considered an intention, as is the feeling that one *ought* to do something. In general, personal dispositions are thought to be the source of intentions.

While the intention linked to an action provides the directional aspect of trying, the quantitative aspect is supplied by *exertion*. Exertion varies directly with the difficulty of the task—our canoeist must paddle more strenuously as the current increases—and inversely with the person's ability—a highly skilled athlete can make his performance look easy by substituting finesse for brute strength. It should be clear that *exertion, ability, task difficulty,* and *luck* are all involved in the production of action. What this means for the perceiver is that a clear attribution to any one of these requires prior knowledge of the others. In the case of successful action, for example, if our canoeist is paddling across a river famed for its swift and dangerous current, and if he succeeds with little apparent exertion, then we can conclude with some confidence that his ability is substantial. If, on the other hand, he succeeds only after strenuous exertion, the attributional conclusion is equivocal: either he does have the necessary ability (and would succeed in the future) or he was just lucky (and might well fail if he tried again). The solution to this attributional problem, is, of course, to have the poor fellow try a repeat performance, on the basis of a judgment that success through luck would not occur twice in a row.

In the case of failure at an attempted action, the attributional problem facing the perceiver is even more difficult. Was the failure a result of a lack of motivation (no trying or, more appropriately, no exertion), or was it a lack of ability? Let's assume that our canoeist doesn't reach the opposite shore (and, so that we may continue to talk about him, that he is fortunately rescued by a powerboat when he is just a few yards short of plunging over the falls). If we have observed him exerting himself to the limit, we could conclude that he just didn't have what it takes. If he appeared to be paddling in a lackadaisical manner, we would conclude that he just didn't care, but here it is difficult to know whether he didn't care even though he did have the necessary ability, or whether he didn't care because halfway across he realized that he had no chance to succeed. Finally, if he was paddling moderately strenuously, this sort of ability-motivation confusion would be even greater. In short, failure leads to an attribution of clear lack of ability only under conditions of high exertion. Under any other circumstances there will be ability-motivation confusion.

LEVELS OF PERSONAL RESPONSIBILITY FOR ACTION

The attributional outcome of the entire naive analysis of action is, of course, a judgment of the extent to which the actor is personally responsible for the occurrence of an event. In a general sense, this attribution of responsibility varies with the relative contribution of environmental and personal force to the action outcome: the greater the environmental contribution, the less the attributed responsibility. Heider outlines five "levels" of interaction between personal and environmental force, indicating the attribution made at each level. The levels have been named by Shaw and Sulzer (1964) and later renamed by Sulzer (1971). They can be described as follows:

1. *Association.* This most primitive level of attribution of responsibility takes place without reference to a naive analysis of action, since the person is held responsible for an event not *causally* connected to him in any way. Examples of this level of attribution are the tendency to "blame sons for the sins of their fathers"; the politician's gambit of holding *all* members of the party in power responsible for the country's problems; and the fact that during the Second World War, immediately after the attack on Pearl Harbor, the United States government imprisoned nearly all people of Japanese ancestry who were living on the west coast of the country.

2. *Causality.* At this level anything caused by the person is ascribed to him. Here the person is a necessary condition for the occurrence of the event and the dispositional state of *can* is present, although neither intention nor motivation is inferred. Indeed, this level of responsibility can be attributed even when the occurrence of the event could not have been foreseen by the actor. For example, consider a motorist in heavy traffic approaching a temporary construction detour around a segment of highway. Failing to see a small dog crossing his path, the motorist strikes the dog as he enters the detour. He looks in his rear-view mirror, can see nothing but cars right behind him, and assumes—since the detour is bumpy—that he has simply hit a sizable rock. The motorist continues, completely unaware that he has caused the animal's death, although this causal link was obvious to a construction worker who observed the accident but was unable to prevent it.

3. *Foreseeability.* At this level of responsibility *can* is also present (the person is a necessary condition for the occurrence of the event), and although neither motivation nor intention is inferred, the perceiver does judge that the actor could have foreseen the occurrence of the event. This is the level of attribution that is typically invoked in the assignment of responsibility for events produced by "carelessness."

4. *Intentionality.* Responsibility is assigned at this level if the naive analysis of action leads the perceiver to judge that *can* obtains, that the person is trying to accomplish the action, and, subsequently, that he had the intention to produce the event. Here the person is seen as almost the sole cause of the occurrence.

5. *Justifiability.* Although the naive analysis of action leads to the conclusion that *can* was present and that the person intended to produce the action and was trying to produce the action, there are

cases of justifiable commission in which the actor's behavior is ascribed to environmental coercion. To employ an example from the law, causing the death of another person by shooting the victim with a pistol can be manslaughter (the level of foreseeability present in the case in which the pistol "was being cleaned"), murder (intentionality—the victim was unarmed and unsuspecting), or self-defense (the victim was an armed intruder and the commission was justifiable).

Heider's attribution theory asserts that the goal of interpersonal perception is an understanding of the *dispositional properties* inherent in the environment and other people that will make the perceiver's world more predictable. When a perceiver is faced with the necessity of interpreting the behavior of another person, he must choose among at least three possible explanations. Was the behavior produced by the situation (so that under similar circumstances in the future it might recur); was it an unintentional or "chance" occurrence (with a correspondingly unpredictable future probability); or was it an intentional behavior reflecting personal disposition (and so might occur in the future, even under different circumstances)? The last of these dispositional attributions provides the perceiver with the most information and requires a prior inference that the behavior was intentionally caused. The degree of personal force entering into production of the behavior can be assessed as shown in Figure 4-2. Given the judgment of personal causality, an attribution to personal disposition is presumed to follow from the effects produced. A more detailed specification of this latter process is provided by the work of Jones and Davis (1965), to which we now turn.

The Correspondent Inference Theory of Jones and Davis

In their attempt to make Heider's theory more amenable to empirical test, Jones and Davis (1965) chose to concentrate on the effects produced by an action. Even though a perceiver does not, in many cases, actually witness an act, he can frequently infer an underlying disposition from knowledge of the effects of the act. In fact, some of the more important interpersonal attributions—for example, those made by psychotherapists, juries, or even presidential commissions—are accomplished by perceivers who have no first-hand knowledge of the behavior to be interpreted. Assuming that unintended effects and effects outside the range of the actor's capabilities are irrelevant to perceivers, Jones and Davis analyzed the

Audyzed

relationship between the effects of an action and the disposition revealed by those effects.

Choices and Effects

Not only is every action presumed to carry with it certain specifiable effects, each unit of intentional behavior can be seen as one of several possible actions available to the actor at the time. Although Jones and Davis do not explicitly say so, an actor could be considered always to have a *choice* between courses of action (even though the choice may sometimes be only between action and inaction). Consider the following example: On a beautiful spring afternoon, I as an actor have several possible courses of action: I can remain in my office as usual, I can go to the library, or I can play tennis with a friend. Each of these behavioral alternatives carries with it a set of possible effects. If I remain in my office, it may be to complete grading some papers, begin work on a new book, or just catch up on some needed reading. I may also have a chance to see an old (but generally unreliable) friend who said that he might be able to stop by my office on his way to the airport. If, as a second possibility, I go to the library, I may accomplish more of the work I had planned, but I might also miss seeing my friend (if he comes). This second course of action also relieves me from the interruptions of students and the telephone. Finally, if I choose to play tennis, I will give my usually sedentary body some needed exercise, will have the stimulation of friendly physical competition, and will enjoy both the game and the beautiful afternoon to the utmost.

Let us assume that I choose to play tennis. How will you, as a perceiver, go about the task of determining whether that behavior reflects an underlying disposition? Each of the three behavioral alternatives carries with it a specified set of effects. For explanatory convenience, Jones and Davis first note the potential effects of each behavior in "choice circles," shown in Figure 4-3. "Stay in Office" will produce a, b, c, and d; "Retreat to Library" will bring about a, b, c, and h; and "Play Tennis" will produce e, f, g, and h. Notice that while an effect produced can be the *absence* of a particular state of affairs—effect h is the absence of interruptions—the choice circles contain only those effects produced, not effects avoided or lost. In principle, effects lost by making a particular choice could be represented in the choice circle, but when all the choices are known (and it is assumed that they are) such a procedure would add no useful information. Indeed, because some effects produced can be negatively valued (few professors place a high positive value on

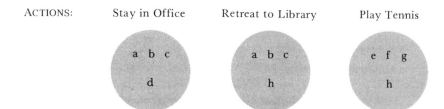

ACTIONS: Stay in Office   Retreat to Library   Play Tennis

a b c   a b c   e f g

d   h   h

EFFECTS:

a complete grading of papers
b begin work on a new book
c catch up on needed reading
d possibly see old (unreliable) friend
e obtain exercise
f gain friendly competition
g enjoy beautiful weather
h avoid interruptions

Figure 4-3. Choice circle analysis of common and noncommon effects of behavioral alternatives. (Adapted from Jones and Davis, 1965.)

grading papers) the attempted inclusion of effects lost in a choice circle already containing negatively valued effects would be almost impossibly confusing. *Not logically consistent.*
Grading papers isn't the effect
Having papers which are graded is the
COMMONALITY AND DESIRABILITY *effect – This may not be*
negatively valued

common

As the next step in the inference process, Jones and Davis assume that effects produced by two or more potential choices cannot have served as the basis for a decision between those possibilities. Since effects a (paper grading), b (begin book), and c (catch up on reading) are *common* to the choices "Stay in Office" and "Retreat to Library," these common effects can not be the basis for a choice between those two behaviors. Similarly, since effect h (avoiding interruptions) is common to "Retreat to Library" and "Play Tennis," it cannot be the reason for a choice between those two alternatives. *goes to Kelley* Only the *noncommon* effects—those unique to each course of action—can be used to infer the reasons for the choice that was actually made. But how are the noncommon effects used in the inference process? According to correspondent inference theory, the first comparison between possible choices is in terms of the *number* of noncommon effects. For example, the choice between Play Tennis and Retreat to Library involves a total of six noncommon effects (a, b, c, e, f, and g) and the choice between Play Tennis and Stay in Office has a total of seven noncommon effects (a, b, c, d, e, f, and g). In contrast, a choice between Stay in Office and Retreat to Library would involve only two noncommon effects (d and h).

After considering the number of noncommon effects involved, the perceiver then attempts to assess the *assumed desirability* of these remaining effects. In making this estimate of assumed desirability, the perceiver may use any of several categories of people for the reference point, and this choice of reference group will have a significant effect on his attribution. As an example, let us consider "beginning to write a new book." Should the perceiver choose the average man on the street as the reference for estimating the desirability of this effect, he might conclude that any actor making a choice that led to that effect had an intense personal desire to be an author. Because "writing books" is not something that just anyone would think desirable, the perceiver would be tempted to conclude that the choice reflects a personal disposition of the actor. But what if the reference group changes from the man on the street to the social category of all college professors? Now the assumed desirability of book writing should increase. Why? Because writing books is something that college professors often do, and it is unlikely that a person would choose to be a college professor if he did not place a high value on writing books (whether or not he ever intended to write one himself). To go further, what if the reference group is "all college professors who have previously written books"? If the perceiver knows that the actor is at a university where nearly everyone writes books, his estimate of the assumed desirability of that behavior will increase even more.

With each change in the reference group, the perceiver learns a little more about the likelihood that the actor would have considered the effect desirable *in advance of the immediate situation*. Jones and Davis refer to this likelihood as the *prior probability* that the effect would be seen as desirable by the reference group in question. Now, what does this knowledge do to the perceiver's attribution? With a reference group of men on the street, recall that the perceiver attributed the choice leading to book writing to a personal disposition of the actor. When the perceiver learns that the actor is at a university where nearly everyone is writing books, the choice sounds less like a reflection of an underlying personal disposition and more like a response to peer pressure (an *environmental* attribution). Under these circumstances, the choice of "playing tennis" begins to reflect a personal disposition, because that activity is more unusual, given the reference group, than is writing books. In other words, the more the actor's choice deviates from what would be expected in the reference group used for comparison, the more that choice will be attributed to a personal disposition.

CORRESPONDENCE OF INFERENCE

Now that we have considered noncommon effects and assumed desirability, we can turn to the perceiver's certainty that the actor's behavior reflects an underlying personal disposition—what Jones and Davis call the perceiver's *correspondence of inference*. High correspondence of inference occurs only with a particular combination of noncommon effects and assumed desirability, and the various possibilities are diagrammed in Figure 4-4. When the number of noncommon effects is high, the attribution of a behavior to a single personal disposition can be ambiguous at best. Alternatively, when the number of noncommon effects is low, the presumed cause of the behavior is clear. When the assumed desirability of the effects achieved is high—when anyone would have tried to produce those effects—very little is learned about the dispositions of that particular actor. When the assumed desirability is low, the behavior is presumed to reflect an underlying disposition that is powerful enough to overcome environmental pressures to do otherwise. The condition of *high correspondence* occurs when there are few noncommon effects, and when the assumed desirability of those effects is low. We can be certain that a politician who advocates achieving cuts in government spending by lowering social security payments to an audience of senior citizens *really* means what he says. If, given only the choice between going to the library and staying in my office, I choose the library, the importance of avoiding interruption (particularly when balanced against the possibility that I may miss seeing a

| | | ASSUMED DESIRABILITY OF EFFECTS | |
		High	Low
NUMBER OF NONCOMMON EFFECTS	High	Trivial Ambiguity	Interesting Ambiguity
	Low	Trivial Clarity	High Correspondence

Figure 4-4. The determination of correspondence of inference from the number and assumed desirability of noncommon effects of action. (Adapted from Jones and Davis, 1965.)

good friend) makes the action sound as though it reflects an underlying disposition of real dedication. In such a case, in which the "act and the underlying disposition presumed to account for it can be similarly described," Jones and Davis (1965, p. 223) assert that high correspondence of inference has been achieved.

The entire inference process is summarized in what Jones and Davis call the "action-attribute paradigm," shown in Figure 4-5. This diagram traces the course of the perceiver's inference from the observed effects of an action to the inferred disposition that the action is presumed to reflect. Of course, it is not necessary for the perceiver himself to have witnessed the effects, as long as they have been observed by someone who reports them to him. Working from the effects back to the disposition, the model assumes that the actor had knowledge of the effects to be produced by his action and had the ability to produce the action. Knowledge and ability are preconditions for inferring intentions from effects, and the intention is itself a precondition for inferring existence of the underlying disposition.

ATTRIBUTIONAL BIAS

Jones and Davis continue and expand upon Heider's recognition that the attribution process may, at times, be distorted by the *Gestaltist view.* perceiver's personal needs. Two manifestations of the perceiver's personal involvement are considered. First, the action observed may have positive or negative consequences for the perceiver—it may be *hedonically relevant.* To return to our earlier example, if you are both the perceiver of my action and the person who has asked me to play tennis (and if you have previously tried to enlist several of our mutual colleagues, all of whom have dutifully and sorrowfully re-

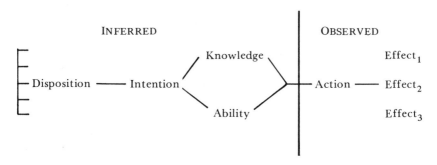

Figure 4-5. The action-attribute paradigm. (Adapted from Jones and Davis, 1965.)

fused to play), then the action I take will be hedonically relevant for you. If I were to refuse, you might not be able to find another potential partner and would lose the opportunity to play, a negatively valued state for yourself.

The second manifestation of personal involvement is derived from a different relation between the action and the perceiver. When the perceiver believes that the action he observes has been uniquely conditioned by his presence, the variable of *personalism* comes into play. If I refuse to play tennis with you on the excuse of going to the library, and then show up at the courts with someone else, you will attribute my refusal to the fact that I simply didn't want to play tennis with you. Particularly when an action is hedonically relevant, a personalistic attribution is likely to be even more extreme.

Jones and Davis suggest how a perceiver searches for the *dispositional cause of an intention*. The perceiver can obtain more information about the actor (1) when the number of effects produced by the action is small rather than large and (2) when those effects are of low rather than high social desirability. In other words, unexpected or *out-of-role* action is more informative than role-prescribed behavior. Finally, the correspondent inference theory suggests how the hedonic relevance of the situation can bias the perceiver's attribution, especially when the perceiver believes that the action was uniquely conditioned by his presence.

The Attribution Theory of Kelley

It is a tribute to the inclusiveness of Heider's original work that Kelley's attribution theory (1967, 1971, 1972) derives from it, as does the correspondent inference theory of Jones and Davis. When Heider was discussing the way in which a perceiver might attribute causality for an event, he suggested that the perceiver might employ a perceptual analogue of J. S. Mill's *method of difference*: the cause for a specific event will most probably be found among the conditions that vary as the event occurs, rather than in the conditions that have been the same before the occurrence and will be the same after the occurrence. For example, let us say that I spend my evenings watching television. I notice that nearly all of the time the picture is excellent, but that occasionally it becomes terrible. I now act not as a naive psychologist, but as a naive television repairman. Is the fault with my set, or is the problem somewhere else? As soon as the picture becomes bad, I quickly change the channel. Now if the bad picture goes away, I conclude that my set is operating properly and that there is "network difficulty." I have varied the conditions—the channel—and have determined that the effect—a bad picture —occurs only in the presence of one network.

This principle of *covariation* between potential causes and effects is the central theme of Kelley's attribution theory, and it is used to explain both attributions made for the behavior of other people and attributions made to oneself for internal feeling states. The theory employs a three-dimensional model, and although Kelley does not say so, it seems reasonable to argue that these three dimensions exhaust the possibilities. In any attribution there will be a *stimulus,* to be placed on Kelley's *entities* dimension; there will be a *perceiver,* included with other people on a *persons* dimension; and there will be a *context* (designated as *time/ modality)* in which the attribution is made. It should be noted that this analysis represents a further partitioning of the environment portion of Heider's *person-environment* dichotomy. —*figure this out.*

The three source dimensions—entities, persons, time/modality —can be considered in the form of a three-dimensional solid (the *attributional data table*) shown in Figure 4-6, and the perceiver is thought to arrive at his attribution by applying the principle of covariation along each of these three dimensions. The theory is perhaps best illustrated by the case of an attribution made for an internal feeling state, and so we will begin with such an example.

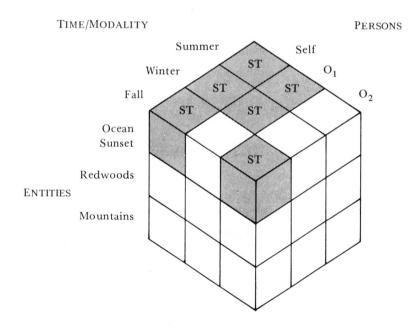

Figure 4-6. Attributional data table representing the attribution of a special thrill from ocean sunsets to the entity. (Adapted from Kelley, 1967.)

Suppose that, although I usually enjoy colorful sunsets, I get a special thrill (ST) from a brilliant sunset over the ocean. Here the ocean sunset is one of the possible *entities* shown in Figure 4-6. Other entities are a forest of redwoods and a mountain landscape. The attributional problem is to account for my special thrill, and we begin by asking whether I am so gushy that I get a thrill from almost anything. In other words, we first apply the principle of covariation along the entities dimension. What we discover is that I do *not* get an ST from either the mountain landscape or the forest of redwoods. In the language of the model, I have a *distinctive* reaction to the sunset, getting the ST in its presence but not in the presence of other scenic entities.

By comparing my reaction to the sunset with my reactions to other entities, we have ruled out lack of discernment on my part as an attributional explanation. But could my ST have come about because the only ocean sunset I have seen was in Hawaii while drinking luscious rum drinks after a great day? In short, was my reaction to the entity or to the context? To answer this question, we apply the principle of covariation along the *time/modality* dimension. If my reaction is the same in the winter in Oregon as it was in Hawaii in the summer (variation in time and place), and if I get the ST while just viewing an excellent color film of an ocean sunset (a change in modality), then my reaction is *consistent* over situations. This consistency allows me to rule out the context as a source of the ST.

There is, however, one remaining alternative to an entity attribution. Perhaps, even though I am relatively discerning about most scenic entities, I just have a "thing" for sunsets. How do I tell whether my ST is shared by others? Apply the principle of covariation again, now along the *persons* dimension. I ask other people whether they get an ST from ocean sunsets. If many of them do, then there is *consensus*: my impression is not unique to me, but rather is shared by other observers.

Having applied the principle of covariation along the three dimensions, I can now rule out all of the alternative attributions and can attribute my ST to the entity: ocean sunsets. It is important to notice that none of the attributional criteria—distinctiveness, consistency, and consensus—needs to be met perfectly for my attribution to be quite stable. My reaction to the ocean sunset does not have to be identical in every situation, nor through every modality, and complete agreement among observers is almost never achieved. The general principle of covariation still applies: the attribution of an effect will be made to a dimension along which there is variation (distinctiveness), rather than to a dimension along which there is little or no variation (consistency, consensus).

To summarize the example, the dimension of *entities* represents things in the environment over which attributional distinctiveness varies. My reaction to sunsets is different from my impression of other aspects of the environment. The dimension of *time/modality* represents the possible modes of interaction between the attributor and his environment, and the time at which that interaction could occur. The third dimension, *persons*, includes the self, the actor (when, in contrast to the present example, the actor is someone other than the self), and other persons whose interaction with the entities forms the basis of consensus. The blocks of this "attributional data table" are the sense impressions, experiences, or responses that enter into the attribution and are necessarily seen from the would-be attributor's viewpoint. (I cannot directly experience the reactions of other persons to ocean sunsets; all I can do is try to understand their impressions as they describe them to me.) Every block labeled with an "ST" indicates that the person in question experiences a "special thrill" when viewing one of the entities at a particular time (through a specified modality). The data table entries show that I (the self) have that reaction only to ocean sunsets, that for me the time/modality changes this reaction only slightly, and that others have similar reactions. Under these circumstances the model predicts, not surprisingly, that I will attribute my reaction to the entity rather than to the time or to some unique characteristic of mine.

ATTRIBUTIONS OF DISPOSITIONS TO OTHERS

Just as the covariation principle can be applied to attributions for internal feeling states, it can be used in the determination of attributions to others. It is important to understand that when the object of perception is another person, that person is represented on the *entities dimension* of the attributional data table. In other words, the entities dimension is used to represent whatever object (be it person, sunset, or something else) is under attributional consideration at the time. For example, suppose that every time I discuss attribution theory with a certain student, we end up in an argument. This situation is represented in Figure 4-7, which shows that the "argumentative student" (you see that I already know how this particular attribution will turn out) is one of the entities. For purposes of comparison, the remaining entities are two other students. The context dimension of time/modality contains possible conversations: attribution theory, music, politics, and the persons dimension includes me and two of my faculty colleagues.

The effect for the occurrence of which an attribution is sought is disagreement, and the attributional data table in Figure 4-7 illustrates where this occurs. Each block of the data table that contains an *A* indicates agreement between a faculty member and a student about a particular topic of conversation; wherever the *D* appears, there is disagreement between a faculty member and a student about a particular topic of conversation. Thus I agree with both other students about attribution theory. My faculty colleague #1 agrees with other student #1 when they talk of attribution theory, and my faculty colleague #2 agrees with both other students when the subject of the conversation is music. In contrast to this pretty picture, the argumentative student and I disagree about attribution theory, he disagrees with faculty colleague #1 about music and politics, and he disagrees with faculty colleague #2 about attribution theory and music so strongly that they never even get to politics. The data table shows that there is a virtual "layer of disagreement" present for the argumentative student.

Now let us return to my specific attributional problem. Is my argument with the argumentative student because of me, because of the topic, or because of him? Considering first the entities dimension, I agree with the other two students, so my reaction to the argumentative student is *distinctive*. Since I cannot stand to talk to the argumentative student about any other topics, I must estimate

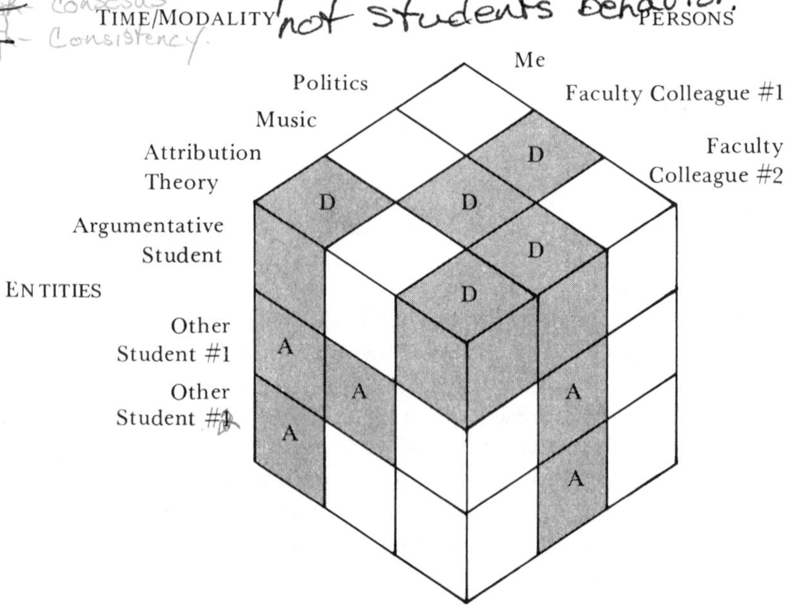

[handwritten margin notes: checking for Attribution to self. High–Dist. Low– Conjesus High– Consistency — professors reaction not students behavior]

Figure 4-7. Attributional data table: disagreeability of actor.

[handwritten note at bottom: Confuses P— Question is professors reaction not students behavior.]

both *consistency* and *consensus* from discussions with my faculty colleagues. I discover that his disagreement is consistent over other topics and, further, that there is consensus in this judgment. Having ruled out possible alternative attributions, I can safely conclude that the effect, disagreement, can be attributed to a personal disposition (argumentativeness) of the troublesome student.

[handwritten margin notes: — No — Can A his reaction to the entity (the person being considered); H - Cons - L; L Consis - H; L Dist - H]

See p.17 - Perspectives - to be Confused.

ATTRIBUTIONAL BIAS

What about potential sources of error in attribution? In addition to those previously mentioned (the hedonic relevance of the situation for the perceiver, the fact that situational constraints on behavior are often overlooked) Kelley also suggests that the *environmental context* of the behavior may be unknown or misleading. A politician who, after believing that he has evaluated all the evidence, votes to continue a sizable tax break for the oil industry may not be aware that most of the material on which his decision was based was actually provided by members of an industry lobbying group. Here the attributional error is not produced by the perceiver's own needs and biases, but rather by the intentional manipulation of the situation by others.

Another source of potential error in attribution is *pluralistic ignorance.* One of the important dimensions for testing the stability of an attribution is, of course, consensus with other persons. If the perceiver cannot engage in this comparison, or if he simply assumes that others will react to a compelling situation in exactly the same way that he will, his attribution may not be veridical. If I had assumed that disagreement with the argumentative student was *his* fault without checking with my colleagues, I could well have been wrong. Since attribution theory is an academic subject, the other two students who agreed with me might have been doing so just to improve their grades. If that were true, then the disagreement might have been a reflection not of argumentativeness but of integrity (or lack thereof). Comparing notes with my colleagues, however, indicates that the argumentative student disagrees with them on music and politics, while other students express agreement when it could not help their grades to do so.

Each of the theories presented in this chapter tries to specify elements of the attribution process. What exactly does a perceiver consider in the course of explaining the occurrence of effects? Heider proposes that the perceiver evaluates the relative contributions of personal force and environmental force, attributing greater responsibility to the actor as his personal contribution is seen to increase. While Heider's naive psychologist considers only actions that have been taken, Jones and Davis's information-processing perceiver is thought to consider also behavioral choices available to the actor but not taken. The number and assumed desirability of the noncommon effects produced by various choices are then assessed to determine correspondence of inference. Kelley's attribution theory extends the coverage to include self-attributions for internal states as well as attributions to other people, and distinguishes between the entities present in the environment and the environmental context in which the perceiver's attribution is made.

5

COMPARISON OF THE
THEORIES

In this chapter we will discuss the conceptual similarities and differences among the attribution theories of Heider, Jones and Davis, and Kelley. After outlining the fundamental assumptions common to all these theories, we turn to comparisons among them at each stage of the attribution process outlined in Chapter 3: observation of action, judgment of intention, and dispositional attribution. The material presented in this chapter can stand apart from the remainder of the book. While the detailed comparisons will be of value to interested readers, many students may want to omit this chapter.

Assumptions of All Theories

In attempting to specify the ways in which human perceivers search for meaning in the behavior of others, the attributional models of Heider (1958), Jones and Davis (1965), and Kelley (1967) rest on three common assumptions. The first of these is the assumption of *minimal determinism* required by any scientific approach to the study of human behavior. There is simply no future in studying regularities in a phenomenon that you believe to be the product of capricious forces, so all psychological theories assume that behavior *it has meaning* is determined in some way. The differences between various theoretical frameworks lie not in the fact of determinism, but rather in the presumed source of the determined behavior. Behavioristic psychology, in the tradition of Skinner, holds that behavior is determined by environmental stimuli; psychoanalysis and other dynamic theories in the tradition of Freud assert the importance of biological factors. At this point in its development, attribution theory does not directly address itself to the ultimate causes of behavior, arguing only that perceivers will believe that, at least some of the time, an actor's overt behavior serves his purposes.

2. A second assumption shared by all attribution theories is that perceivers, themselves, have some reason to engage in a search for the causes of an actor's behavior. Just as the general motivational principle expressed in the first assumption implies that the actor's behavior can be the means toward his ends, it also suggests that the act of attributing serves the ends of the perceiver. Perceivers are thought to have a need to explain and predict, if not control, events of importance to them (especially when these events are the behaviors of other people), and the assumption of *utility* holds that the attribution of specific actions to underlying dispositions helps satisfy this need.

3. Finally, all attribution theories assume that the underlying causes of an actor's behavior can be inferred with some degree of validity from an examination of his actions. This assumption of *validity* should not be taken to imply that there will always be perfect correspondence between the inference made and the "real" causes of the action. Indeed, all theories suggest important sources of bias in such inferences. Not only can observers simply be mistaken, they can distort their attributions to conform to their own personal needs and they often underestimate the environmental constraints on action. On the other hand, if the perceiver's guess is correct only in a substantial fraction of cases, his perceptual tasks of explanation and prediction will be simplified enough to justify his effort.

The Philosopher, the Information Processor, and the Social Scientist

Although the three models share a conception of the perceiver as a basically rational problem solver, there are some important differences in both the presumed nature of his task and the information considered relevant and available. For example, at the risk of oversimplification, Heider's ideal perceiver can be thought of as a *philosopher*, using nothing but the rules of logic to determine from the *content* of an action whether attribution to a personal disposition is appropriate. The important question is, "What must a perceiver consider before attributing a given action to an underlying personal disposition?" If the person's ability seems greater than the task difficulty, and if his exertion in the direction of a presumed intention is greater than zero, then the perceiver must ordinarily conclude that the action arose out of a personal disposition. Notice that this is essentially a binary decision: if the requisite conditions (intention, exertion, *can*) hold, there will be personal attribution; if these condition do not hold, the attribution will be to unspecified aspects of the environment. In addition, the attribution by Heider's ideal perceiver is based almost entirely on the action given and considers neither other actions that might have been possible nor the judgments of other perceivers.

If Heider's perceiver can be considered a philosopher logically assessing the content of an action, the ideal perceiver for Jones and Davis can be thought of as a highly disciplined *information processor.* Restricting their focus to cases in which attribution to personal disposition is appropriate, Jones and Davis ask, "What are the basic steps in the *process* of dispositional attribution?" Their information processor evaluates the action taken in terms of the possibilities available, identifies the common and noncommon effects, assesses the social desirability of these effects, and assumes that the actor was attempting to maximize his outcomes through the action that he took. To the extent that this action differs from the response that an appropriate reference group would have to the same circumstances, the perceiver has learned an important bit of information about the unique character of the actor. Like Heider's philosopher, Jones and Davis's information processor makes an initial binary decision (personal disposition or not), although he does try to distinguish among the several dispositions that might have given rise to the observed action. Another similarity between the two models is that Jones and Davis's perceiver also arrives at his decision in the absence of information from other persons.

In contrast, Kelley's ideal peceiver is a *social scientist* whose task is to locate the source of an event by considering, among other things, the judgments of other persons. Here the important question is, "How can an attribution to a personal disposition be distinguished with subjective *validity* from an attribution to some other source?" The answer to this question is determined by Mill's method of difference—an event is attributed to whatever conditions (be they entities, persons, or situations) vary with the presence or absence of the event. Thus the attribution is not a binary one, since the environment is now partitioned into stimuli (entities) and context (time/modality), and since an essential aspect of the process is the comparison of one's own experience with the experience of other perceivers.

It should be emphasized that the distinctions between perceiver as philosopher, information processor, and social scientist illustrate only differences in theoretical focus, not fundamental theoretical incompatibility. Each of the later theories has borrowed heavily from

Heider, and all three employ many of the same terms in their descriptions of attributional behavior. The most comprehensive attribution theory would undoubtedly contain elements from all three approaches: A thorough understanding of attribution requires consideration of situational variations and consensus, study of the elements of action, and knowledge of the process of inference.

For a more detailed comparison of the three models we now return to the fundamentals of attribution outlined in Chapter 3: observation of the action, judgment of intention, and dispositional attribution. Specific questions will be posed under each of these headings to illustrate other similarities and differences between the three attributional models.

Observation of Action

There is general agreement among the three theories that any attributionally meaningful action must be the joint consequence of personal and environmental forces. The necessity for participation of a person in an action outcome is not intended to deny the existence of events produced entirely by the environment—natural disasters all too often attest to the effects on people of an uncontrolled environment—but merely to suggest that the causes of such events are of no attributional value. Certainly a community's reaction to a natural disaster can tell us something about the community and its residents, but only an occasional fanatic would argue that the fact of the disaster carried implications about the character of the community that was affected. In a similar way, the necessity for participation of the environment is not intended to deny the possibility of purely mental events not accessible to outside observers, but only asserts that such events are not attributionally meaningful. The environment must be either a source of stimuli for an internal event, a factor that enters into the possibility of action, or the object of an action before the perceiver can make a valid attribution. Thus, all three theories define action in terms of *change in the environment* (behaviors that are intended but not successfully executed would be called "attempted actions"), and all three assume that action is the joint consequence of *personal and environmental forces.*

WHAT ARE THE PERSONAL COMPONENTS OF ACTION?

Differences among the three approaches begin to emerge when personal and environmental forces are subdivided into their respective components. Beginning with personal force, Heider delineated three essentials for the production of attributionally meaningful action: *intention, exertion,* and *ability.* Remember that ability combines in an additive manner with task difficulty (the dispositional element of environmental force) to determine whether an action can be performed. If the person's ability is greater than the environmental force opposing action (or if the environmental force is such that it actually facilitates action by a person who otherwise would not possess the requisite ability) then the state of *can* is presumed to obtain. Then the conjunction of intention and exertion determines whether the action will be performed. Intention and exertion are believed to combine in a multiplicative manner, since the action will not occur if either one of these factors has a value of zero.

Jones and Davis agree with Heider that intention is an essential personal component of action, but their model differs from his in two respects. First, it contains no explicit parallel to Heider's motivational concept of exertion. Instead, Jones and Davis assert that the actor had prior *knowledge* of the effects of various actions and then chose an action whose effects would benefit him. In other words, knowledge combines with a guiding principle of utilitarianism to provide the motivation for action. The second difference between the two conceptions of personal force deals with the meaning of the term *ability.* For Heider, ability meant only personal power or skill, and did not of itself indicate whether action could be performed: the possibility of action was determined by the state of *can.* For Jones and Davis, however, the term *ability* does refer to the possibility of action. Their *ability* is identical to Heider's *can.*

It is difficult to extend this comparison to Kelley's model, because with the sole exception of *intention* it contains no specification of any elements that we have been calling personal components of action. While Jones and Davis extend Heider's reasoning by specifying in more detail how a perceiver might choose among several possible *personal* dispositions as the source of an observed action, Kelley extends Heider's analysis by specifying in more detail the various possible *environmental* influences on action. Given a particular observed action to explain, Jones and Davis would ask, "If that action was not a product of the situation, to which personal disposition should it be attributed?" Under the same circumstances Kelley would ask, "If that action was not caused by a personal disposition, to which aspect of the environment should it be attributed?" Thus, while Kelley gives general approval to Jones and Davis's personal components of ability, assumed desirability, and knowledge of consequences, he does not specify any *additional* personal factors thought to account for action.

Just as all theories suggest what elements are required for an attribution to a personal disposition, they also indicate factors in the environment whose presence might preclude a personal attribution. Again we begin with Heider, who identified *task difficulty* as the principal component of environmental force. This stable dispositional property of the environment interacts with ability to determine *can*, and in some cases its effect is augmented or reduced by the variable dispositional properties of *opportunity* and *luck*. Although Heider's theory often characterizes task difficulty, opportunity, and luck as restraints against performance of intended behaviors, it also shows how they can be combined to make possible an action that might otherwise not be performed. In short, there can be both difficult tasks (or bad luck) that must be overcome for successful action, and easy tasks (or good luck) that would permit success by anyone who made the slightest effort. Not only can the environment aid in the production of some desired actions, it can sometimes compel behavior that goes against the actor's wishes. The classic example of this *environmental coercion* is the use of torture to obtain "confessions" from prisoners of war. The power of such coercion is recognized in the last of Heider's five levels for attribution of responsibility —justifiability—in which even the actor's intentional behaviors are not attributed to him. In summary, a completed action will not be attributed to a personal disposition when the task is ridiculously easy, when there is environmental coercion, or when there is evidence of "good luck."

Jones and Davis refer to task difficulty and luck in the same way that Heider does, and they add to the category of coercion another source of environmental influence on behavior, the *prescriptions* of situation and role. Indeed, only to the extent that the actor's behavior deviates from these constraints can a correspondent inference be made about his underlying personal dispositions. This is not to say that all normative behavior is personally uninformative, because in many cases the actor's *prior choices* have determined which set of normative prescriptions apply to him. Recall the example of the professor choosing among staying in his office, going to the library, or playing tennis. Through his prior choices, a professor at a university where everyone writes books has determined that the normative prescription "Write books!" should apply to him. Even if he *follows* this directive (rather than playing tennis) we know more about him than about the average man on the street. Now, although we have learned from his *prior* choices, the *present* choice of the professor (when that choice is to write rather than to play) is normatively prescribed and reveals nothing *more* about his personal dispositions. Thus, in addition to good luck and task simplicity, for Jones and Davis an action will be attributed to the environment rather than to a personal disposition to the extent that the action produced numerous normatively prescribed effects. — *normative effects*

Kelley's attribution theory identifies three major components of the environment that may influence action: *entities* that happen to be present, the *situation* (time/modality) or circumstances in which the action is observed to occur, and other *persons* (usually only the perceiver, but in some cases others as well) who are party to the action. Although Kelley does not specify how his dimensions of the environment correspond to Heider's, it is reasonable to believe that *opportunity* should most probably be considered as an aspect of the situation, while *task difficulty* and *luck* might be entities that could influence action. Normative prescriptions for behavior might be represented either in the opinions of other persons or as part of the definition of the situation.

Although the dimensions (entities, time/modality, and persons) may be used to characterize the environment, the presence of environmental *coercion* (in the form of either irresistible incentive or irresistible prescription) can best be identified using the attributional criteria of distinctiveness, consistency, and consensus. When an observed action is low in *distinctiveness* (almost everyone would have done the same thing under similar circumstances), is high in consistency (relatively constant over time and situation), and occurs in the presence of obviously relevant entities (luck, rewards, punishments), there will be an attribution to environmental forces rather than to underlying personal dispositions. The advantage of Kelley's model over the other two lies in the degree of specificity of such environmental attributions. Use of the attributional criteria permits environmental attributions to varying combinations of entity, situation, or persons. In all of these cases, of course, the guiding principle is *covariation:* An action will be attributed to a component of the environment (entity, situation, target person), rather than to a personal disposition of the actor, to the extent that the action occurs consistently in the presence of that aspect of the environment and not in its absence.

Confusing consensus w/distinctiveness

Co-variation

WHAT IS THE CONTEXT OF ACTION?

Of course, all of the theories require that the perceiver become aware (by direct observation or second hand) that an action has occurred. There are, however, some important differences in the amount of additional information that is presumed to be accessible to the perceiver. As noted above, Heider's perceiver is thought to arrive at his attribution through a logical analysis of the *action as it is given:* little additional information is available. Specifically, the environmental context of the action is included as part of the data for the attribution, but other possible actions are not dealt with.

This stands in direct contrast to the model proposed by Jones and Davis, which suggests that all action can be conceived of as *a choice between the action taken and other actions thought to be possible.* This choice serves as the basis for the calculation of noncommon effects (effects of the action taken that would not also be achieved by other actions possible), and these noncommon effects form the core of the process of attributing an underlying personal disposition from an action. How are the "other possible actions" determined? Under the best of conditions, the several choices available to the actor would be explicitly stated by him to the perceiver but, of course, this occurs only rarely. More typically the perceiver must guess what choices were available to the actor, drawing on his own experience as an actor in similar circumstances. It is important to notice that this extension of the context is not accomplished without some penalty—the perceiver's guesses about other actions available to the actor can be colored by his own personal needs in a way that a simpler view of the action could not. Indeed, the variables of *hedonic relevance* and *personalism* provide a place in the theory for just such motivated distortions of the attributional process.

Although this choice among behavior alternatives plays a smaller role in Kelley's overall framework than in Jones and Davis's correspondent inference theory, the fact of such choice is implicit in the attributional data presumed to be available to the perceiver. The question is not so much "Does the perceiver consider what else the actor might have done?" as "How can that guess be made more accurate?" Here again the attributional criteria come into play. An accurate assessment of the possibilities open to the actor requires at least (1) knowledge of what capabilities the actor has and (2) some evidence that the particular perceiver's assessment of the situation is not a unique one. Observation of the actor under a variety of situations (to determine *consistency* and *distinctiveness*) will help delineate what the actor is capable of doing. Now, instead of having to guess whether the actor can perform a certain action in the abstract, the perceiver is in a position to know whether such an action has been performed under other circumstances or at another time. In addition, the comparison with others that helps establish *consensus* will point out any cases in which the perceiver's view of the situation differs from the view held by others. Finally, consideration of time, situation, and other perceivers present provides a more precise specification of the action context than is contained in either of the other two theories.

Judgment of Intention

WHAT IS THE PLACE OF INTENTION IN THE ATTRIBUTION PROCESS?

For each of the three models, intention is a crucial element in the attribution of underlying personal dispositions from observed behaviors. Heider (1958, p. 100) called intention "the central factor in personal causality," a description that Jones and Davis, and Kelley also support. As pointed out in Chapter 3, belief by the perceiver that the actor has some purpose (intention) in performing the action must precede any attempt to understand which of the several dispositional possibilities actually brought about the behavior. The logical necessity for an inference of intention to precede any dispositional attribution does not imply (again, as Heider illustrated) that the actor need be conscious of his intentions.

WHAT ARE THE FEATURES OF INTENTIONAL ACTION?

How is the perceiver to decide whether an action was intentional or accidental? What are the clues employed to make the inference of intention? For Heider three factors enter into this determination: equifinality, local causality, and exertion. — intention

The notion of equifinality refers to the fact that the statement of a person's intention is a statement of his *goals* rather than a statement about the particular *means* that might be used to obtain those goals. For example, since the end of the process is the most important, if one manner of reaching the goal is blocked or thwarted another path will be sought, and this process will continue until the goal is finally reached. A person who intends to travel from Norfolk, Virginia, to Washington, D.C., may first try to take the train. Discovering that the train no longer makes such a run, the person may attempt to fly via the commercial airlines but, finding the pilots to be on strike, he may decide to drive his own automobile. Finally, when he learns that road construction has closed the major highways, so that he would have to detour through Chicago, he might just give up on the usual forms of transportation and use a boat to sail up the Chesapeake Bay and Potomac River. Although the number of alternative paths chosen will depend as much on the strength of the intention as on its presence, the fact that each path terminates in the same place illustrates the principle of equifinality.

Equifinality alone, however, is not sufficient to distinguish personal causality from the impersonal causality found in some physical systems. For example, a river originating east of the Continental Divide will flow east toward the Atlantic Ocean regardless of the obstacles placed in its path (such as hydroelectric power plants) and although in certain areas it may double back on itself and temporarily flow westward. This is an equifinality determined at the outset, at a considerable distance from the origin, and with no additional intervention along the way. In contrast, the person performing an intentional action is present at its beginning, intervenes when necessary to redirect the action toward its goal, and is present at the end, acting as a truly *local cause* throughout.

While equifinality and local causality are sufficient to distinguish personal causality from impersonal causality, the perceiver needs information about exertion in order to make judgment of intention. In other words, it is possible to have personal causality of an accidental or unintended nature. A person who steps on a board placed between two high buildings is certainly the cause of the board's breaking, but few perceivers would infer that this outcome was intended. Not only were there good reasons for not breaking the board (such as the resulting five-story fall), but if that had been the actor's intention, there were numerous better ways to carry it out. Thus, the first step in the analysis of the actor's exertion is a judgment of whether the actor's exertion seems to be in a direction that is *appropriate* to accomplish the potential intention. Following this judgment, the perceiver can examine the degree of exertion. Was the person who intended to break the board tapping it lightly with his hand, or was he vigorously swinging a sledgehammer at it? Intentions will be inferred even if the action is appropriate only above certain minimal levels of exertion. Below this cutoff point, the perceiver will say that the actor was merely "faking" the exertion in order to maintain the appearance of having the intention.

To summarize, personal causality is distinguished from impersonal causality by equifinality and local causality, and within personal causality intentional action is distinguished from accident by the presence of exertion.

The correspondent inference model of Jones and Davis begins consideration of intentional action only after the question of personal versus impersonal causality has been settled: since the action and its effects were observed to be associated with the person, the only problem remaining for the perceiver is "to determine which of these effects, if any, were intended by the actor" (1965, p. 220). The necessary preconditions for a judgment of intention are the presumptions by the perceiver that (1) the actor had the ability to carry out his intentions and (2) he knew the consequences of his action. Both of these can differentiate intentional action from accidental personal causality. Beginning with ability, remember that Jones and Davis use this term to refer to the actor's capability to perform the action, a state roughly equivalent to Heider's state of *can*. Since ability when defined in this way includes not only personal power but also environmental force, the judgment that the actor possesses the requisite ability implies a capability that is relatively stable despite either opposition or assistance from the environment. If you are judged to have the ability to paddle your canoe across the river, then you are considered capable of performing that action without the help of a strong wind at your back and in spite of the swift current of the river. Bad luck should not deter you, and good luck should not be necessary. — *this is not necessarily true* —

Ability may be determined in a context not as an absolute.

Turning to knowledge of consequences, Jones and Davis point out that only those effects that could have been foreseen by the actor are attributionally informative. Unforeseen consequences are, by definition, excluded from the set of effects that could have been intended. This does not mean that all effects must be foreseen *consciously*, although Jones and Davis prefer to concentrate on conscious intentions. Nor does the exclusion of unforeseen effects from the basic attributional data relieve the actor of the responsibility for unintended consequences of his actions. For example, the fact that involuntary manslaughter carries criminal penalties illustrates that such judgments of responsibility are often made. All that the exclusion of unforeseen effects does is restrict the class of attributionally useful effects to those that might have been intended by the actor. Thus, in Jones and Davis's terms, accidents are characterized by judgments of low ability and low knowledge of consequences.

According to Kelley's attribution theory, as in the analysis by Jones and Davis, the perceiver's task begins after the issue of personal versus impersonal causality has been settled. The action to be interpreted is *given* as associated with the actor, and the important question is not the fact of that association but the reason for its existence. Specifically, was the action the product of an underlying personal disposition, or was it the result of some aspect of environmental force (entity, situation, or person)? As usual, an attribution of personal disposition must follow an attribution of intention, and the model suggests how a perceiver might evaluate these attributional dimensions in order to make the judgment of intention.

First, intentional action can be distinguished from habit or idiosyncrasy by simultaneous consideration of the dimensions of *situation* and *person* (the actor) to estimate the number of actions possible. The perceiver can simply enumerate the other behaviors available to the actor in that situation. In principle, this enumeration can be accomplished either by recollection of things that the actor has actually done in past similar circumstances, or by generalizations that the perceiver makes from his own experience. If the actor is thought to have a large number of alternatives available, then he will most probably be seen as having intentionally chosen among them. If, however, his behavior in the past has been constant in similar circumstances, the action will most likely be interpreted as habitual.

Next, intentional action can be differentiated from accidental personal causality by analysis of the *entities* dimension. As pointed out earlier, task difficulty and luck may properly be considered entities that can affect the behavioral outcome. Then, as the model suggests, an attribution of an action to an intention arising from a personal disposition will be made to the extent that entities in the environment do not appear to have produced the action. In other words, attributions to meaningful intentions will be the only remaining possibility after all potential environmental causes have been ruled out.

Dispositional Attribution

What is an Underlying Personal Disposition?

As this concept is used in each attribution theory, it seems to have three relatively distinct meanings: descriptive, predictive, and causal. First, an attributed personal disposition can be seen as characterizing or *describing* the overt action from which it is inferred. You will recall that this sense of the term forms the basis for Jones and Davis's concept of correspondence of inference: "the extent that the act and the underlying characteristic or attribute are similarly described" (1965, p. 223). Returning to the fistfight in the park (Chapter 3), the perceiver's attribution of hostility to the assailant also serves to characterize the action (as opposed to, for example, a description of that act as an accident). In much the same way, other adjectives can be used to describe both an action and an underlying disposition reflected in the action—skillful, friendly, authoritarian, dogmatic, etc.

The second sense in which personal dispositions are employed is a *predictive* one: the dispositional attribution carries implications about the future probability of action that would not follow from a description of the action alone. To assert that an overt action reflects an underlying disposition of friendliness is to believe that similar actions are highly likely to occur in the future. Certainly this potential for similar action in the future is limited by the circumstances (not even the most friendly people are *always* pleasant), and just as certainly there will be differences between people in the degree of friendliness attributed to them. A single, isolated friendly action may reflect the disposition, may be an act of flattery, or may be a disguise for hatred, and the existence of these possibilities reduces the accuracy of any attempt to predict for the future. The perceptual act of making the dispositional attribution, however, consists of ruling out some of these alternatives and results in a corresponding increase in the reliability of prediction.

Finally, a dispositional attribution is usually given the conceptual status of a *causal* factor that influences behavior. Why did the assailant attack the other man in the park? *Because* he was a hostile person. To both the lay perceiver and the attribution theorist this explanation is, as Heider would say, "sufficient." In other words, when an overt action is attributed to an underlying personal disposition, that disposition is seen as the cause of the action as if the actor were only incidental to the process. This causal power of the disposition is perhaps best illustrated by the legal defense of insanity. An actor who commits a violent crime with greatly heightened passion and without premeditation can under some circumstances claim to be innocent by reason of temporary insanity. The personal disposition of insanity (over which the actor presumably has no control) is claimed as the cause of the criminal action in an explicit denial of personal responsibility. Thus, not only can environmental factors be held responsible for intentional behavior (in the case of coercion), but the internal personal dispositions of actors can also diminish responsibility and blameworthiness.

It should be noted that this causal usage of personal dispositions represents what some philosophers, notably Ryle (1949), refer to as a *category mistake*. The argument goes like this: When we think of the category called "causes of events," we normally think of *persons* (often, as the attribution models illustrate, to the exclusion of relevant environmental factors). How may the category be described? Well, since persons are observable entities composed of matter which occupy space and are capable of directing action to influence the environment, it would be reasonable to assert that causes of events should have these same characteristics. Now consider the characteristics of underlying personal dispositions: they are *not* observable, are *not* composed of matter, do *not* occupy space, and can produce changes in the environment only with the mediation of a person. If personal dispositions and persons are considered equivalent in the category of causes of action, then a cause could either be composed of matter or not, could occupy space or not, could be directly observable or not, and could directly produce environmental change or not. Under these circumstances it would be nearly impossible to exclude *anything*. If the category "causes of events" is to have meaning, we must be able to identify *both those things that belong in it and those things that do not belong*, and making dispositions equivalent to persons has completely precluded such decisions. As a result, we must conclude that it is a mistake in logic to place the two into the same category.

The fact that causal usage of personal dispositions is a logical mistake does not, of course, preclude perceivers from making such attributions, any more than the knowledge that some attributions can be distorted will end all such distortion. Attribution is a *psychological* process that may or may not be entirely rational, and it is clear that perceivers do attribute some behavior to enduring personal dispositions presumed to exist apart from the overt actions that can be observed.

As an attributional example of the category mistake, consider the similarities and differences between having your leg broken and having a nervous breakdown. To begin with some similarities, both involve a reduced level of activity, both can engender compassion from others, and both can be treated (although with different "crutches"). Now the crucial attributional difference: once healed, the physical injury is thought of as "cured," regardless of its initial severity. In contrast, the psychological injury is often considered to have left some residue even though all symptoms have disappeared. While we would never consider describing you as "an ex-broken leg," we might very well refer to you as "an ex-mental patient." The disposition of being physically sick vanishes with the end of the symptoms; the disposition of being mentally sick remains even in the absence of any observable signs. When the surgeon informs us that the broken leg is not only healed but as strong as ever, we accept his conclusion at face value. On the other hand, no matter how many psychiatrists or psychologists state that the psychological damage is repaired, we are apt to believe that you have hidden within you a disposition toward mental breakdown. Because perceivers do make this and other such category mistakes, an attribution theory that tries to describe the perceiver's processes will also include that possibility. Recognition of the problem will, however, simplify discussion of some theoretical problems to be encountered later.

[Handwritten margin notes:] lot a good analogy — broken leg + mental breakdown = different losses of events. mental breakdown usually implies inherent weakness in system — broken leg doesn't.

What is the Link Between Intention and Dispositional Attribution?

The purpose of any attribution is to account for the occurrence of a specific action. The process begins with the action and terminates when a sufficient explanation for its occurrence has been provided by an attribution either to immediate environmental forces (task difficulty, luck, situational prescriptions, environmental coercion) or to a personal disposition. For the latter to occur, there must be a prior inference that the actor *intended* to perform the behavior that was observed. Thus all three theories recognize that a judgment of intention is a necessary precondition for a personal attribution, and differ only in the degree to which they hold intention to be sufficient for personal attribution.

At one extreme is Heider's position that intention, of itself, is not sufficient for dispositional attribution. In the case of actions that could be considered desirable, there must be exertion in the direction of the intention as well as the intention itself. If an action occurs with intention but with only minimal exertion (perhaps aided by the environment), no attribution to personal disposition should result. In the case of action considered undesirable, a personal disposition will not be attributed to an actor whose intentional behavior appears to have been forced by coercion of the environment. The position taken by Jones and Davis occupies the middle ground: there is no specific requirement for exertion, but personal dispositions are not likely to be attributed for actions that produce numerous highly desirable effects. When the effects produced are less constrained by the situations, any intentional action is attributed to personal disposition regardless of the amount of exertion. The other extreme is represented by Kelley's restriction of the class of intentional actions to include *only* those that do not appear environmentally constrained. In other words, while Jones and Davis would argue that intentional action to obtain highly desirable effects is attributionally uninformative, Kelley would not even call such action intentional. Consequently, any behavior considered intentional in his scheme is automatically a product of a personal disposition.

Is Dispositional Attribution the End of the Process?

Remember that in Chapter 3 we suggested that it would be possible for a perceiver to decide first that a specific action was the manifestation of an underlying personal disposition and then to inquire about the possible sources of that disposition. Is the convicted burglar really an incorrigible thief by nature (in a sense, was he born that way?), or is his apparent personal disposition the result of his environment and life experiences? This search for potential environmental sources of dispositions must not be confused with the environmental attributions that can be made for specific actions. Indeed, all of the three theories permit the latter while ignoring the former. Knowing that the source of the actor's thieving nature was a psychological trauma suffered in childhood may make the perceiver more sympathetic, but that knowledge adds little to the description of the specific action and less to the perceiver's ability to predict whether it will be repeated. Finally, since there is the psychological tendency to see the personal disposition as the cause of the behavior, any change in the thief's life history would presumably be reflected in his personal dispositions before it would affect his behavior. Thus, while the failure to go beyond the personal disposition is a shortcoming of all three theories, it is not surprising given the objective of accounting for the occurrence of specific actions.

6

ATTRIBUTIONS TO SELF

In the preceding chapters we have traced the development of an identifiable body of attribution theory from the broader area of person perception; outlined the three principal models of attribution proposed by Heider (1958), Jones and Davis (1965), and Kelley (1967); and compared the ways in which these models deal with the observation of actions, the determination of intention, and the making of dispositional attributions. So much for the major theoretical notions. Now, how can the general approach of attribution help you to reach a more thorough understanding of your social world? Since understanding should perhaps begin with you, this, the first of the more applied chapters, deals with self-perception.

We have repeatedly argued that a perceiver's attempt to understand the world of human behavior will lead him finally to dispositional attributions that will at once explain actions that have occurred and predict the likelihood of the recurrence of these actions. At times these attributed dispositions can appear to take on causal properties, and nowhere is this possibility more frequently realized than in attributions made to the self. Most of us have a subjective experience of volition, of being in the position to make choices among various behavioral alternatives, and our everyday language reflects that subjective experience. Whether it is a young child proudly acclaiming that he has accomplished a task "all by myself," or an elderly mystic achieving Nirvana through intense contemplation of his inner experience, it is typical to refer to _the self_ as if it were an independent, tangible object capable of causation.

Despite the dubious philosophical status of the self-as-causal-agent, most psychological controversy has centered not on whether the self is an identifiable entity but on what sort of entity it is and how knowledge about that entity is obtained. What is the influence of personal motivation on self-awareness? Do the presumed causes

[handwritten margin note: maybe necessary Cause for some events]

of your own behavior differ from the causes you believe to underlie the behavior of others? How well do you really know yourself? Traditional notions of self-concept, beginning with that of William James, and theories of self-knowledge, such as symbolic interactionism (Mead, 1934) and social comparison (Festinger, 1954), suggest that were it not for your own motivation toward self-enhancement you would know yourself fairly well. In rather direct contrast, attributional analyses by Jones and Nisbett (1971) and Bem (1967, 1972), which concentrate on cognitive factors, suggest more limited self-knowledge. Bem's self-perception theory even asserts, somewhat surprisingly, that you do not know what you think or feel until you see what you do.

The present chapter begins with consideration of traditional notions of self-concept, continues with more recent developments in attribution theory, and concludes with discussion of some enduring individual differences in degree of self-attribution. For example, a large part of your social behavior may be related to what deCharms (1968) has called the *origin-pawn* dimension of self-concept, also described by Rotter (1966) in terms of *locus of control*: Do you believe that the important things in your life are under your personal control, or are they instead under the control of external forces? Careful consideration of some of these issues may give you a new outlook on some of your own behavior.

Traditional Conceptions of the Self

THE ME AND THE I

One of the earliest distinctions drawn about the nature of the self was the difference between self-as-object (the *Me*) and self-as-subject (the *I*) described by William James (1892). The *Me* is defined as *the sum total of all that a person can call his own* and consists of three major components: the constituents of the *Me*, the emotions to which those constituents give rise, and the acts that result from these emotions. The class of constituents may be subdivided into three parts: the material self, the social selves, and the spiritual self. The material self is a single category thought to include the person's body, his clothes, his home, and his other material possessions. Each of these items is said to be part of the person's material self. In a similar manner, the spiritual self is a single constituent category that includes all of the person's psychological faculties and dispositions. For example, sensation, conceptual ability, and verbal skills are all part of the person's spiritual self. Finally, there is the multiple category containing all of the person's social selves, and it is assumed that there is a separate social self for every outside person who recognizes the individual and carries his image in mind.

In short, while there is a single material self and a single spiritual self, there are multiple social selves. The existence of multiple social selves is a recognition that the person can occupy several different roles: "As a host for a cocktail party you are charming, but I would never buy a used car from you." Although the social selves are separate, no one of them is unique, because each shares at least some common elements with others. In addition, the roles which an individual plays can differ greatly in importance to him. If your lover thinks the social self that he or she sees is wonderful, your employer's evaluation of your "employee social self" may matter very little.

The second component of the *Me* consists of the emotions to which the constituents give rise. If your possessions are increasing, you feel happy about it (unless you have adopted an antimaterialistic life style); if you lose everything, you are crushed. You delight in the spring smell of honeysuckle, unless your nose is stopped up with a cold. If all around you are singing your praises, you can't hear enough; but if no one has a good word to say about you, you have already heard too much. James considers these emotions to fall into two broad classes: *self-complacency* (pride, arrogance), and *self-dissatisfaction* (humility, despair).

The final component of the *Me* consists of the two sets of acts that are produced by the constituents of the *Me* (and sometimes by the emotions to which those constituents give rise). First among these are the acts that serve to maintain the present state of the self. These acts of *self-preservation* can be purely physical activities—reflex actions, bodily self-defense—or aspects of social interaction designed to maintain the integrity of the social and spiritual selves. If, through an unpleasant interchange with another person, you suffer a heavy blow to one of your social selves, you may very well need to spend some recuperative time alone (almost literally to "pull yourself together") before plunging back into the social world. The second general set of actions, characterized as *self-seeking*, consists of behaviors designed to provide for the future rather than merely to maintain the present. Once again both physical activities (storing of food, contributing to Social Security) and social experience (enlarging your circle of acquaintances, learning how to win friends and influence people) can be involved.

This description of the objective content of the self, the *Me*, is important for our purposes not only for the structure of self that it implies, but also for the motivational influences it permits. The structural division of the *Me* into material, social, and spiritual selves is an organization reflected both in later psychological theories, such as Maslow's hierarchy of personal needs (1954), and in various aspects of popular American culture. For example, if you'll forgive some oversimplification, it could be argued that the materialism produced as a reaction to the Depression gave way, when affluence was achieved, first to a concern for authentic interpersonal (social) contact, exemplified by the interest in encounter groups, and then more recently to a return to inner (spiritual) experience through meditation. Not only is the structure of the *Me* preserved in later psychological theories, the motivational concepts of self-seeking and self-preservation can be seen even more specifically as influences on attributions. After all, the reason that affective significance, hedonic relevance, and personalism can produce distortions in attribution is simply that they have consequences for self-seeking and self-preservation.

If the *Me* is the sum total of the content of the self, then the *I* can be considered the ongoing process of consciousness. It is the pure ego, the thinker, the knower, or, as James calls it, the organized *stream of consciousness*. Since the *I* is a process rather than a collection of empirical entities (like the *Me*), it is exceedingly difficult to describe in concrete terms. While the *I* can peruse and consider the objects of consciousness, it is not an aggregate of those objects; while it can be thought of as participating in the direction of purposeful behavior, it need not be considered "an unchanging metaphysical entity like the Soul, or a principle like the transcendental Ego" existing apart from time and space (James, 1892, p. 215). In other words, by referring to the *I* as the passing stream of consciousness, some of which may be recollection of former times and places, James avoids making the *category mistake:* The *I* is not endowed with the qualities of an enduring entity and is not thought to be a separate causal force apart from consciousness. Rather, it *is* the dynamic process of consciousness, the awareness of self and of individuality.

SYMBOLIC INTERACTIONISM AND THE LOOKING-GLASS SELF

Of the constituents of self proposed by James, the social *Me* is the most essential for attribution theory. The *I* and the spiritual *Me* are aspects of self to which only the individual has ready access, so it is impossible to measure, for example, the consistency of self-attributions in these areas. On the other hand, while the material *Me* is readily observable to others, this high visibility renders almost trivial any attributions constructed on material possessions alone. Theoretically more interesting questions can be framed around the fact that one's social self (as expressed in the interaction) will differ depending on who is watching, and around the observation that even with the particular perceivers held constant, one's own self-perceptions may differ greatly from the perceivers' impressions.

Early interest in the relationship between self and other perceivers can be found in the sociological tradition that has come to be known as *symbolic interactionism* (beginning with Cooley, 1902). As compared to the psychological foundations of attribution theory that focus on the individual perceiver, this more social view concentrates on interactions between two perceivers—self and other. Despite this difference in viewpoint, symbolic interactionism rests on many of the assumptions that also serve as support for attribution theory. For example, a basic presumption of symbolic interactionism is that people exist in a symbolic environment where even physical objects assume importance primarily because of their *social meaning*. A building is not important because of its physical description—walls, floor, roof, windows, doors, etc., all of specified shapes, sizes, and colors—but because of its social function as a gathering place for people. Similarly, the importance of a social interaction is derived not from, say, the physical description of linguistic elements transmitted between participants, but rather from what those linguistic elements *mean* to the participants. And, of course, one of the goals of attribution theory is to explain the ways in which the participating individuals search for these social meanings.

A second basic presumption of symbolic interactionism is that the social meanings of objects in the symbolic environment can be described in *value* terms (basically, positive and negative) from the standpoint of the perceiver. A conservationist may agree with the developer of a recreation area that the social meaning of a building constructed in a wilderness area will be "increased public use of that area," but the two can be expected to disagree on the value of that meaning. Again, attribution theory attempts to specify classes of personal needs and motives that may lead to such different assignments of value to a single social meaning.

So far we have been speaking of meanings and values as if each person independently constructed these aspects of the symbolic environment in the absence of any communication with other people. That, of course, is not the case. Indeed, the "interaction" part of symbolic interactionism specifically considers the fact that people do communicate with each other and as a result of this symbolic interaction *learn* the meanings ascribed and the values held by others. Because we share a common language and have the ability for symbolic thought, we can, at least in principle, put aside our parochial concerns and look at the world from the perspective of other perceivers. Not that we do this sort of thing all of the time, or even often enough. Nevertheless, the conservationist can *understand* the developer's viewpoint (and vice versa) even though he may not agree with it.

The communication inherent in symbolic interaction has two important consequences for the development of the self-concept. The first of these is the expansion of your own horizons that follows the exposure to the ideas, experiences, and values of other people. Good novels let us see the world through another person's eyes, films let us experience places (and, vicariously, emotions) that we might not otherwise discover, and as McLuhan (1964) has argued, the immediacy of mass electronic communications can produce "worldwide community" through simultaneous experience of important events. All of these involve what an early interactionist, Mead (1934), called *taking the role of the other*. We can learn to develop empathy for each other by symbolically stepping into each others shoes.

The second important element in symbolic communication is an extension of the act of taking the role of the other. If I look at the world through the eyes of the people around me, one of the things that I will see is, obviously, myself. The social meaning of my behavior will be assigned a value by those around me, and that value will be reflected in their actions toward me. Not surprisingly, Cooley (1902) described the resulting picture as a "looking-glass self." I can symbolically put myself in the other's position to determine what sort of impression I am making. "What do you think of me?" is a very interesting question, made even more so by the relative infrequency with which it is directly asked. Indeed, many of our interactive behaviors are designed not so much to obtain an accurate answer to the question as to produce a self-presentation that will guarantee a positive evaluation. In other words, the looking-glass is a bit tarnished with self-seeking. I am not, therefore, confused in my self-concept if I behave totally differently around my parents than I do around my close friends. Even if the two performances are completely inconsistent, *I* still know which is the *real* me; I am simply trying to avoid unpleasantness. Fundamental changes in my self-concept will occur only if I can find no one who will place a positive value on my actions when I am not putting on a face.

SOCIAL COMPARISON PROCESSES

In the ideas of the symbolic interactionists we begin to see how I might learn of the evaluations that others place on my social *Me*. We also get an inkling of the possibilities for bias in self-knowledge through the motivation of self-seeking. Both of these processes may be more specifically described in terms of social comparison theory (Festinger, 1954). In short, we need a bridge between the complete set of social selves suggested by James (and implied in the looking-glass concept) and the specific behaviors of interest to attribution theory. Social comparison can provide that bridge. Although the theory is quite detailed, for our purposes it can be summarized in three basic propositions: that people have a drive to evaluate their opinions and abilities; that in the absence of objective information this need can be satisfied by comparison with other persons; and that these comparisons will be made, when possible, with people similar to the self.

social comparison theory

In some interesting ways social comparison theory can be regarded as a more specific, and more psychologically oriented, version of symbolic interactionism. For example, to provide the framework for distinguishing between objective and social comparison, Festinger (1954) first described a *physical reality* of time and space that contains objects whose characteristics can be relatively unequivocally specified. This physical reality is essentially the same as the symbolic interactionist's physical environment. In contrast to the physical reality is a *social reality,* an interpersonal world of subjective judgments, that is analogous to the symbolic environment. To illustrate the difference between objective and social comparison, suppose that I believe (1) that the moon is made of green cheese, and (2) that people's privacy should be respected by the government no matter who the people are. The first of these opinions can be checked against physical reality (provided that I can talk the astronauts out of some of their moon rocks). There is no corresponding method for ascertaining the validity of the second belief, so all I can do is ask other people for their opinion on the matter. While this process of social comparison is not quite the same as taking the role of the other, it does involve similar interpersonal sensitivity. I must be able to take another's view at least enough to know whether he is similar to me on attributes related to the comparison.

Why must I choose a similar other for social comparison? In order to answer this question we need first to consider the meaning of the term *evaluate.* In doing so, we may see other similarities between social comparison and symbolic interactionism. As Wheeler (1970) and others have pointed out, the postulated drive to evaluate opinions and abilities can be separated into two components. Evaluate could mean "find the location of," and in that sense I could assess my belief in privacy by determining which people on various dimensions of the political spectrum agree or disagree with it. A second possible meaning, not unrelated to the first, is "place a positive or negative value upon." This valuing process is exactly the same as the one described by symbolic interactionists. Now, why do I choose a similar other? For reasons associated with both senses of evaluate. If my only interest is locating the belief, the best estimate will be obtained from people who differ only slightly from me, or better yet, who are nearly the same except for a single possibly relevant dimension. If I am an over-thirty professor of social psychology, and I discover that self-confessed violent anarchists also want privacy, I don't know whether it is because they agree with the principle, or whether they simply don't want their bomb factory discovered. Since I am not interested in the practical value of the belief but only in its place in abstract political philosophy, comparison with an anarchist provides little useful information. If, on the other hand, I am interested in having my self-esteem enhanced by being congratulated for holding the belief, then a similar comparison-other who would be most sympathetic to my view is the best choice.

Social comparison theory makes two important contributions to the traditional conception of self-concept. First, it outlines a dynamic process that can account for the development and change of attitudinal constituents of the self. When a comparison with similar others leads to satisfactory evaluation (in either sense of the term), opinions become more stable; when the comparison is unsatisfactory (unstable or negatively valued), the person will be open to attitudinal change. Second, it identifies an interpersonal behavior—choice of a comparison-other—that can interact with self-seeking to bias the self-concept. Continual choice of similar others for social comparison will reduce the likelihood of encountering discrepant information from people with different views. In addition, if valuation of the belief becomes more important than determining its correct location, even the minimal similarity sought may change from "relevant attributes" to "identical biases." Like so many other processes, social comparison is a potentially useful explanatory device, but one whose operation can be adversely affected by needs of self-preservation and self-enhancement.

Actors and Observers:
More than a Difference in Viewpoint

Recall that in Chapter 3 we outlined the three stages of the attribution process: observation of action, judgment of intention, and dispositional attribution. If we consider the perceiver's task at each of these stages, we might think that there should be some important differences between attributions made to other actors and attributions made to the self. When you try to answer the question "Why did I do that?" you ought to have full knowledge of the situational demands to which you are responding, you ought to be able accurately to identify the intention behind your action, and you ought to know whether that intention was the product of a momentary whim or of one of your underlying personal dispositions. At each step in the process, you *should* have more complete information than would be available to any outside perceiver of your actions.

What makes this situation especially intriguing is the observation that a relatively high frequency of people seem not to be in touch with their own dispositions, despite their presumably more complete information. We can all think of examples: There is the ingratiating and obsequious student, whose ulterior motives are obvious to both teachers and fellow students but who resolutely insists that he is simply interested in the subject matter. There is the politician whose positions on important issues change drastically depending upon the immediate audience. We think him power-hungry and Machiavellian, but he says he is merely serving the interests of his constituency. In these other cases, we as outside observers are likely to believe that such persons are deceiving themselves, but it is possible that their view of their actions really does differ from ours.

Some of the reasons for the actor-observer differences in attribution have been discussed by Jones and Nisbett (1971), who argue that there is a *"pervasive tendency for actors to attribute their actions to situational requirements, whereas observers tend to attribute the same actions to stable personal dispositions"* (p. 2). In addition to differences in information about the immediate situation (causal factors in the environment, the actor's intentions and feeling states), the actor and observer bring quite discrepant degrees of personal history to bear on the attribution. The observer often bases his attribution primarily on contemporary behavior rather than on history. In contrast, the actor has at his command a vast store of personalized history against which he may judge his current actions. An excellent example of the differences produced by history comes from studies of the attribution of ability (to be more fully described in Chapter 8). If I ask you to perform a task that presumably measures your intelligence and you fail miserably, you are more likely to question the validity of my test than the level of your intelligence. You have a lot of experience with your own intellectual capability and are not going to change your entire self-concept on the basis of a single failure in a contrived situation. If, however, I ask you to evaluate the intellectual capability of a person you have never met (telling you only that he has failed my test), then unless you have taken the test yourself you most probably will decide that the stimulus person is not very bright. You make a situational attribution for yourself, and a dispositional attribution for the other person.

A second major source of actor-observer differences suggested by Jones and Nisbett is the potential for differential processing of the information that is available. The observer is attending not to the causal factors in the situation but to the actions of the stimulus person (the actor). In Heider's terms (1958, p. 54), the actor's behavior "has such salient properties that it tends to engulf the total field," putting situational constraints into the background. For the actor, however, the focus of attention is precisely those situational factors ignored by the observer. Unless you are an incredible egotist, always "performing" rather than being yourself, you are not going to be highly conscious of your own behavior. Thus, given the difference in attention and perspective, it is not at all surprising that the actor and the observer arrive at opposite causal attributions. The magician succeeds in dumbfounding his audience not because the hand is quicker than the eye, but because the hand knows where it is going.

Self-perception as a Cognitive Process

It is important to note that the work by Jones and Nisbett signals a shift in emphasis from earlier conceptions of the self and self-perception. Whereas James speaks of motives of self-seeking and self-preservation, and the symbolic interactionists assume that motivation will play at least a minor part in taking the role of the other, and social comparison theory is based on a drive to evaluate, the mechanisms outlined by Jones and Nisbett are fundamentally *cognitive* rather than motivational. The actor who attempts to understand his behavior is seen not as a self-enhancer or self-protector but as a dispassionate processor of information. His view of his behavior differs from that of an outside observer not because of motivational distortion but because of a difference in perspective. The most complete statement of this cognitive view of self-attribution is the self-perception theory of Bem (1967, 1972).

According to this theory, "individuals come to 'know' their own attitudes, emotions, and other internal states partially by inferring them from observations of their own overt behavior and/or the circumstances in which this behavior occurs" (1972, p. 2). The self-observing actor is, within the informational constraints outlined by Jones and Nisbett, thought to be in the same position as the external observer. In other words, you do not know what you think or feel until you see what you do. At first blush, this analysis appears to contradict our intuitive belief that people have relatively stable attitudes that do not change capriciously from one moment to the next. On closer examination, self-perception theory deals not with the simple presence or absence of an attitude, but rather with the process of attitude formation and the degree of commitment to a formed attitude. I know that I am opposed to crime without having to observe my behavior. Or do I? Just *how* opposed to crime am I? Have I discussed the problem with my friends, written to my congressman, actively participated in local organizations designed to alleviate some of the social conditions which contribute to criminal behavior? Even the traditional characterization of an attitude as containing cognitive, affective, and *behavioral* components suggests that my behavior is an accurate predictor of my attitudes. I may, in fact, be able to learn more about the strength of my conviction by observing my behavior than by any other activity.

DISSONANCE STUDIES

Self-observation is an especially valuable source of information about attitudes when relevant internal cues are ambiguous or lacking, and such instances provide most of the experimental evidence in favor of the theory. While the evidence is not conclusive, self-perception theory suggests plausible alternative explanations for phenomena usually associated with the motivational theory of cognitive dissonance (Festinger, 1957). As you probably know, this theory (not to be confused with Festinger's social comparison theory) argues that people strive to maintain consistency among their attitudes, values, *cognitive* and representations of their behaviors (all referred to as "cognitive *dissonance* elements"). If for some reason an inconsistency develops—you participate in a terribly boring psychology experiment but then tell another subject that the experiment was interesting—you experience *dissonance* that is unpleasant and must be reduced. One of the major strengths of dissonance theory has been its ability to make "nonobvious" predictions, but Bem's self-perception theory appears to render some of these findings obvious.

As an example, let us consider the classic dissonance experiment by Festinger and Carlsmith (1959). You have agreed to participate in a psychology experiment and arrive for your appointment. The experimenter brings you into a laboratory room containing the apparatus, an elevated platform with several rows of holes, each hole containing a peg. Your task is to turn each peg exactly one-quarter turn to the right. When you finish with the last row, you are to begin all over again. After an almost intolerable twenty minutes, the experimenter tells you to stop and explains that you were in an experiment designed to assess the effect of prior instructions on performance of a motor task. Since you were in the control group, you received no prior instructions, but the next subject to be run (now sitting in the waiting room) is to be told that the task is highly enjoyable. Unfortunately—and here comes the manipulation—the experimenter's usual assistant has not shown up, so he wonders whether you would agree to give the "enjoyable and interesting" description to the next subject. For your help the experimenter agrees to pay you either $1 or $20. Virtually no subjects refuse to help, and after each gives his description to the waiting subject (actually a confederate of the experimenter) he is asked to indicate how much he, personally, enjoyed the task. Subjects who received $1 for their false description said that they found the task more enjoyable than did subjects paid $20. This nonobvious finding was interpreted by Festinger and Carlsmith as evidence for the motivation of dissonance reduction. Subjects who had been paid only a small amount for giving false testimony to the waiting subject were considered to be experiencing an unpleasant conflict. The small payment is *insufficient justification* for the lie involved. One of the best ways to resolve this conflict is to change your private attitude to agree with the public statement that you made to the waiting subject.

This study and several others in the same tradition generated a great deal of controversy in social psychology because the results contradict what would be expected on the basis of reinforcement theory. A person's attitude should change more the *more* you pay him to adopt a new position, not the *less* you pay him. It is interesting to note that both sides in this incentive versus reverse-incentive controversy base their arguments on motivational principles, while Bem's reinterpretation of the insufficient justification studies argues that *no* motivation was involved. His analysis goes like this: You participate in the boring task, but even after your experience with it your attitude toward the task remains ambiguous. It certainly was not the most interesting experience you have had, but it wasn't the worst, either. Now if you tell another subject (for a payment of $20) that the task is interesting, you will see your action as determined primarily by the external reward—not by your internal attitude toward the task. If, however, you perform the same action for payment of $1, the payment is not powerful enough to get you to lie, so your attitude toward the task can't be all that negative. Finally, when the experimenter asks you to indicate your "true attitude," you observe your behavior and the external variables (payments) controlling that behavior exactly as would another perceiver. What must your attitude be, given that you were willing to describe the experience as enjoyable for such a small (large) reward?

Because the dissonance and self-perception interpretations differ only in terms of whether motivational intervening variables are assumed, it is obviously difficult to distinguish between them until the presence or absence of motivation can be tested convincingly in some direct (e.g., physiological) manner. Thus, although Bem's analysis is simpler (and so preferred), better experimental evidence for self-perception comes from studies of oversufficient justification (Nisbett and Valins, 1971), for which the two approaches make different predictions. The insufficient justification paradigm utilizes a small extrinsic payment for a counterattitudinal behavior, while the oversufficient justification paradigm involves a large extrinsic payment for a *proattitudinal* behavior. Because this proattitudinal behavior is something that you would do anyway with or without reward, giving you a reward for performing the behavior cannot possibly be thought to produce dissonance. But, as Nisbett and Valins point out, the self-perception analysis is exactly the same as in the case of insufficient justification. In either instance the subject is pictured as examining the reinforcements available to determine whether his behavior is under the control of external rewards or of internal attitudes. Now it is the self-perception theory that leads to the nonobvious prediction: The more you pay a person to do what he would do anyway, the *less* favorable toward that activity his private attitude becomes.

An interesting experiment that supports this view has been reported by Lepper, Greene, and Nisbett (1973). Nursery-school children were first given the opportunity to play with felt-tipped pens and high-quality drawing paper to establish a baseline level of intrinsic interest in these materials. Children who met the criterion for intrinsic interest were then assigned to one of three experimental conditions: Expected Reward, Unexpected Reward, and Control. Then, in a group drawing session, each group was given an additional opportunity to use the materials. Prior to the session the Expected Reward group members were told that they would receive "Good Player" awards for drawing pictures; no advance instructions were given to either of the other groups. After the session both the Expected Reward and the Unexpected Reward subjects received "Good Player" awards. Several days later all children were once again allowed to use the drawing materials as part of the free play in the nursery school while observers recorded the percentage of time spent with them. As predicted, children in the Expected Reward group played with the drawing materials only about half as much as children in the other two groups. Should these findings that extrinsic reward can apparently undermine intrinsic motivation continue to be replicated, they would have substantial implications not only for the development of self-perception theory but also for the widespread educational and social uses of extrinsic rewards.

EMOTIONAL AROUSAL

A final area in which Bem's self-perception principles find application is the area of emotional arousal and awareness. How, for example, do you know that you are frightened? The first theoretical answer to this question was proposed by James and Länge (1922) and suggested that the subjective experience of emotion was the consequence, rather than the antecedent, of behavior: you are afraid *because* you are running (specifically, because of the visceral changes brought about by the action of running). But because of evidence that the viscera are slow to respond, that emotional states can be demonstrated in animals whose neural connections to visceral organs have been severed, and that people have difficulty distinguishing between several emotional states solely on the basis of visceral cues, Cannon (1929) proposed an alternate theory that asserted that both the visceral cues and the subjective experience of emotion are the product of the activation of certain portions of the brain. You are running *and* and you are afraid because you are activated. Finally, because of evidence that different emotional experiences can be induced given the same physiological arousal, Schachter (1964) proposed a cognitive-physiological theory of emotional arousal: you are afraid because you are aroused and because there are stimuli in the environment that serve as cognitive cues for fear. The classic experiment of Schachter and Singer (1962) on which the cognitive-physiological theory is based deserves more detailed comment, both because of its importance to that theory and because variations of its design have been interpreted in terms of Bem's self-perception theory as well.

In order to simulate the physiological arousal that usually accompanies emotion, Schachter and Singer injected their subjects with epinephrine (adrenaline). Such an injection produces subjective feelings of heart palpitations, hand tremor, rapid breathing, and a warm feeling of flushing. All subjects had been led to believe that the injection was an experimental vitamin supplement, but some (the Informed group) were told that all these symptoms were side effects of the vitamin drug. When the symptoms did occur, then, the Informed subjects would have an appropriate (and completely internal) attribution for their subjective feelings. A second group of subjects (the Ignorant group) was simply given the injection with no prior warning about the symptoms to follow, and a third (Misinformed) group was told that the vitamin drug did have side effects but that these were numbness, itching, and slight headache (all obviously inappropriate to explain the symptoms to be produced). The Misinformed group was included as a control against later emotional differences based solely on physiological introspection, and a second control group was injected with saline solution and was given no instructions.

There is usually a three- to five-minute delay before symptom onset with the dosage of epinephrine used, and during this interval each subject was joined by an experimental confederate who had been trained to act either in an angry manner or in an euphoric manner. Thus, for those subjects without an adequate explanation for their impending symptoms the social actions of this confederate could provide an appropriate cognitive label. Since the Misinformed subjects were intended only as an additional control, they were exposed only to the euphoric confederate. As a result, the euphoric confederate was seen by two groups (Ignorant and Misinformed) that should have had arousal but no appropriate label for that arousal and by one group (Informed) that should have had an appropriate label. The angry confederate was seen by one group without a label (the Ignorant group) and one group with a label (the Informed group). The results of the study strongly confirmed the predictions: When the confederate was angry, the Ignorant group reported more subjective anger than did the Informed group; when the confederate was euphoric, the Ignorant and Misinformed groups reported more euphoria than did the Informed group.

To put these results in Bem's terms, the person evaluates his internal state and the circumstances in which that state occurs in order to "decide" what his subjective emotional experience will be. It should be noted that this "decision"—like the self-interpretation of attitudes described earlier—need not be one of which the person is aware. Bem's analysis does not require conscious participation of the person any more than, say, Kelley's attribution theory requires conscious judgments about behavioral distinctiveness. When there is an appropriate internal attribution for the subjective feeling—"The drug is making me feel this way"—the confederate's behavior has little influence on the subject. In contrast, when there is no label or the label is inappropriate, the social context created by the confederate suggests a possible attribution that is adopted by the subject.

Later research in this tradition also provides support for Bem's analysis and has demonstrated that people can be induced to misattribute not only the source of their physiological arousal but also the

[handwritten margin note: to explain his feeling wants to know the cause —]

degree of arousal. Nisbett and Schachter (1966) studied the source of arousal by giving subjects an increasingly intense series of shocks after the subjects had received a placebo pill. Half of the subjects were led to expect autonomic arousal as a side effect of the pill (providing an alternative label for fear of the shock), and these subjects showed much greater shock tolerance before reporting pain. Ross, Rodin, and Zimbardo (1969) obtained similar misattributions of fear using intense noise rather than an ingested drug as the alternative source of arousal, and they suggested that this "induced cognitive misattribution" paradigm might have therapeutic benefits. Storms and Nisbett (1970) did find therapeutic uses for induced misattribution, and we shall return to this topic in Chapter 9. Finally, a study by Shaver, Turnbull, and Sterling (1973) suggests that a similar cognitive misattribution process may be involved in choice of a dangerous occupation.

Turning to the degree of arousal, several studies reveal that people can be induced both to overestimate and to underestimate their level of physiological arousal. In the first of these studies, Valins (1966) showed slides of female nudes to male undergraduate students who had been attached to dummy electrodes. These electrodes ostensibly measured the subject's heart rate, which was then played back to him over a loudspeaker. On a randomly selected few of the slides this programmed heart rate either increased or decreased appreciably, remaining virtually unchanged on the other slides. Attractiveness ratings of the slides were obtained as each was shown, and at the conclusion of the series subjects were told that they could take a few of the slides with them. On both the attractiveness ratings and the slide choices subjects showed definite preferences for slides on which there had been heart rate change, regardless of whether that change had been an increase or a decrease.

Apparently, subjects can be misled into believing that they have been emotionally aroused by a stimulus. Interestingly enough, the reverse also appears to be true. In a similar false heart rate study, Valins and Ray (1967) showed slides of snakes and of the word *shock* (accompanied by a mild shock to the fingers) to people who were afraid of snakes. Here the programmed heart rate changed on the shock slides but not on the snake slides. After this procedure, experimental subjects (who believed the heart rate to be their own) were able to approach a small boa constrictor more closely than were control subjects who had been through the same procedure but did not believe the heart beat to be their own. In a related program of research, Lazarus (1966) has found that various kinds of externally provided coping mechanisms can reduce the emotional response to stress and that these strategies are most effective with subjects predisposed to defend themselves in the manner suggested. We shall return to this material again in Chapter 9.

We shall return to this material again in Chapter 9.

Cognition or Motivation?

The induced cognitive misattribution studies show, rather paradoxically, how an essentially cognitive approach like Bem's can be invoked to explain subjective experiences of emotion and motivation. Does this mean that we can discard the concept of motivation entirely when we discuss self-awareness? Certainly not. We can still find, in the experimental laboratory and in the real world, enough examples of blatant self-enhancement and self-preservation to support a belief in motivational influence on self-perception. In an important sense, to ask "Cognition or motivation?" is to ask the wrong question: self-perception is neither purely cognitive nor purely motivational, but rather contains substantial elements of both. What self-perception theory, as well as other attribution theories, has done is to rekindle an interest in cognitive and phenomenological processes. When we ask a person to describe his social self we will still be obtaining, in part, his dissonance reductions, his rationalizations, and his self-enhancements, but we will also be getting a personal description of his phenomenology. This will differ from time to time and from person to person, but self-perception theory suggests that there will be some common cognitive themes.

Individual Differences in Self-perception

The attributional analysis of self-perception suggests that the circumstances under which various behaviors occur will help to shape the subjective experience of attitude or emotion. The examples used to illustrate this position have dealt almost exclusively with isolated situations occurring within relatively short periods of time. But if a person can learn about the relative contributions of his internal states and external forces to a single behavior by observing an isolated situation, it follows that he might develop a generalized estimate of these relative contributions by making observations across situations and over time. In addition, because people's life experiences are different we might predict that people would develop different generalized estimates. People with early successful experiences in controlling aspects of their environment would come to expect success in the future, while people with early failures in affecting the environment might continue to expect failure. Finally, if these early experiences served to establish the person's category (remember the prior-entry effect), the generalized expectancy might persist despite later evidence to the contrary. This analysis is an oversimplified version of the position known as *social learning theory* (Rotter, 1954) and shows how people might develop what Rotter (1966) calls *generalized expectancies for internal versus external locus of control of reinforcement.*

Do the reinforcements (both rewards and punishments) that we get, especially in social situations, appear to be capriciously dispensed by factors external to ourselves regardless of our behavior, or are those reinforcements instead regularly contingent on our actions? Because of differences in socialization, it is reasonable to expect that individuals might vary along a continuum from belief in highly internal control to belief in highly external control. In an attempt to measure these individual differences, Liverant, Rotter, and Crowne (reported in Rotter, 1966) developed a forced-choice scale consisting of 23 pairs of statements, such as:

a. What happens to me is my own doing.
b. Sometimes I feel that I don't have enough control over the direction my life is taking.

For each pair, the subject is asked to choose which member of the pair he believes to be more true. As you can see, within each pair one statement suggests that reinforcements are contingent on behavior, while the other statement implies that reinforcements come capriciously from the environment. An individual's score on the test is computed by assigning a point whenever the external choice is selected, and these points are simply added together to create the final score.

Internal-external locus of control has been found to be related to socioeconomic class (Battle and Rotter, 1963), with lower classes expressing fewer internal attitudes than middle-class groups. It also appears to be related to socialization experiences (Katkovsky, Crandall, and Good, 1967), with protective and approving parental behavior associated with more internal scores by children. These results suggest, as do interracial comparisons on locus of control, that beliefs measured by the scale do in fact reflect life experiences. For example, studies show black people to be more "external" than whites, even with social class controlled (Battle and Rotter, 1963; Lefcourt and Ladwig, 1965). Interestingly enough, for both whites (McGhee and Crandall, 1968) and blacks (Coleman et al., 1966) locus of control seems highly related to academic achievement, with "internals" achieving at higher levels than "externals."

Although most of the locus of control data show substantial consistency, a number of people have recently suggested that internal-external is probably not a unitary dimension (e.g., Gurin, Gurin,

Lao, and Beattie, 1969). For instance, it is one thing to believe in internal control when the question is one of responsibility for successes, and quite another when the issue is blame for failures. Whether you express internal or external control may thus depend on the specific question. Another potentially meaningful distinction can be drawn among possible reasons for stating external beliefs. The fact that there is greater behavioral variability associated with external scores led Hersch and Scheibe (1967) to argue that we should consider both how much a person might need to believe in external control and whether he thinks that control will be benevolent or malevolent. Obviously, if you think that Fate will smile upon you, you should leave yourself in Fate's hands. If, however, you fear a malevolent system, then you had better look out for yourself. Finally, on the internal end of the scale, it is a good idea to distinguish between general statements of a Protestant ethic sort ("People who work hard will be rewarded for it") and statements of personal efficacy. You may have discovered that, because of your particular life situation, the Protestant ethic that works for others does not have the same relevance for you.

[handwritten margin note: would seem to not hold due to class + race studies]

A slightly different approach to individual differences in internal versus external attributions is exemplified by the work of deCharms (1968) on the *origin-pawn* dimension of felt (or perceived) subjective volition. Internal-external locus of control presumably represents a relatively stable personal disposition, while origin-pawn is primarily a means of classifying the actions of an individual (sometimes self, sometimes other) who is responding to a specific situation. Degree of "originship" assigned by you to yourself or to another will affect your perceptions of that stimulus person. When you believe another person to have originated an action that harms you or your interests, your evaluation of him will be much more negative than if you believe that he was merely the tool of forces beyond his control. To be told by the underworld hit man, just prior to being rubbed out, that it "ain't personal" is supposed to make you feel better.

Degree of originship has implications not only for interpersonal perception but also for self-satisfaction and persuasibility. If you believe that you are primarily responsible for the completion of a task, you will be more satisfied with the result than if you have been guided every step of the way. This principle, is, of course, nothing new to the generations of industrial psychologists who have been trying to "humanize" assembly-line production. Loss of individual autonomy to the relentless procession of the line is a major cause of the dehumanization that needs to be corrected. As other research reported by deCharms indicates, there can be variations in felt or attributed originship which depend on the nature of the agent directing your behavior, even if the amount of direction is the same. For example, you see a person who complies with the demands of a large institution as more of a pawn than one who complies with a small group. Again, the stereotypical view of the assembly line seems relevant. What could more perfectly represent the impersonal power of a large institution? Even in the military there is more opportunity for individual freedom of action. Thus, it is not surprising that more positive work-related attitudes are developed when employees are given the chance to complete a whole product, working in groups as small as possible, with participation in the decisions that affect them. All of these factors can contribute to the feelings of personal efficacy (originship) necessary for the maintenance of self-esteem.

In this chapter we have considered some traditional views of self-knowledge, a more cognitive attributional view of self-perception, and some possible ways in which individuals may differ in ascribing their behavior to internal or external forces. Perhaps the best summary of this material is to say that self-perception can involve a little of everything. When we are unsure of our beliefs and emotions, we may well learn what we think by observing what we do. When the beliefs we express are closely tied to maintenance of self-esteem, our impressions are likely to be biased by our motivation. And finally, there are relatively enduring individual differences in self-attribution that can interact with motivation and circumstances. Attempts at thorough self-knowledge will require consideration of all of these factors.

7

ATTRIBUTIONS TO OTHERS: CAUSALITY AND RESPONSIBILITY

What should be more obvious to you as a perceiver than the causes of your own behavior? Yet we have just seen how your perceptions of your actions can vary depending upon the degree to which you believe your attitudes and emotional reactions to be determined primarily by internal causes or by forces in the external environment. Even when you should have the most reliable information, you can be misled about the source and degree of emotional arousal and about the source of attitudes. Certainly it is true that these mistakes are made when your internal cues are ambiguous, but the point to remember is that the number of ambiguous cases can only be greater for attributions to others than it is for attributions to self. With that caveat in mind, let us turn to the most fundamental interpersonal attributions: causality and responsibility.

Some Definitional Problems

We often speak as though causality and responsibility were unambiguously related to each other, with personal responsibility for any action following in a necessary way from a judgment of personal causality. If you behave in a manner that causes injury to another person, you will be held responsible for that injury. Or will you? What if the injury is the result of a violent rage, itself the product of a passing emotional disorder? Under these conditions, we typically separate causality from responsibility: "not guilty by reason of temporary insanity." In other words, responsibility (in the sense of being held legally accountable or punishable for action) does not always follow from causality. Should we stop with this example, we might conclude that the group of actions for which you can be held responsible is *smaller* than the number of actions you cause.

It would be tempting to leave the definitions at this point and move on to attributions, but that would be a mistake. Consider another example, again drawn from legal concepts of responsibility. Suppose that your 14-year-old child throws a brick through a school window. Whatever damage there is will not be assessed directly against your child, who is a minor, but rather against you. In a legal sense, you will be responsible. This is true in part because if it had not been for you and your spouse there would have been no errant child to engage in vandalism. Just the same, the child's throwing a brick at the window, in Heider's terms, was clearly more of a local cause than was your act of procreation. If we had considered this example alone, we might have concluded that the set of actions for which a person can be held responsible is *larger* than the set of effects for which he is the local cause. This obvious contradiction suggests that, before proceeding, we need to examine more closely the possible meanings of causality and responsibility.

CAUSALITY   Dif btw causality/resp

Looking first at the issue of causality, there are several dimensions that can be used to characterize a person's causal participation in the production of effects. The previous example suggests the first of these, *local versus remote participation.* Did the stimulus person actually produce the effect, either alone or in concert with other people, or was he merely associated in some way with the real actor? The responsibility (putting aside, for the moment, exactly what we mean by that) assigned to the stimulus person should be greater the more his local participation.

A second dimension on which causality can be characterized is *foreseeability,* the degree to which the effects produced could have been known to the actor in advance of his action. This dimension applies primarily to instances of local causality, and can be represented as a continuum that runs from zero foreseeability through probable to complete foreseeability. For those events classified at the low end of the continuum, we should keep in mind potential differences between foreseeability to actors and to observers, since we can think of instances of causality—like the skier producing the avalanche—not foreseen by the actor but readily apparent to observers. For events falling in the middle of this continuum, most perceivers would agree that the actor should have been able to identify most of the direct consequences of his behavior and many of the unintended side effects as well. In legal terms, this degree of foreseeability might translate into what is known as the "reasonable man" standard: The consequences of action would have been foreseen by any reasonable and prudent person who contemplated the situation. Finally, at the upper end of the dimension all intended consequences would be obvious and most unintended side effects should also be discernible. Presumption of this level of foreknowledge is usually required for judgments of premeditation.

With other aspects of the situation holding constant, the amount of responsibility assigned to an actor should vary with the degree of perceived foreseeability. To use the terminology of Heider's levels again, local causality accompanied by low foreseeability best represents Causality. When potential foreknowledge increases to the middle of the continuum, we reach the level of Foreseeability. At the upper end of the scale, complete foreknowledge might lead to an attribution of Intentionality. Usually implicit in the level of Intentionality is the presumption that there is a desire to produce the effects that are the consequents of action. If a person has complete foreknowledge of the consequences and performs the action, the best statistical prediction would be that the actor desired those effects.

That this is not always the case suggests a third dimension of causality: *environmental coercion*. As Heider points out, a person is not held responsible even for intentional behavior when coerced (Justifiability) on the grounds that the true cause does not reflect an enduring personal disposition. Notice that this characterization of causality includes both causes outside the person and temporary states of emotional disorder (defense by reason of insanity). Coercion from the environment does not make the behavior any less locally caused by the actor or any less intentional, only less blameworthy.

Responsibility

Throughout the preceding discussion of causality, we have spoken of responsibility as if it were a unitary concept with an unequivocal definition. Unfortunately, this is not the case. Just as it was necessary to distinguish among various senses of causality, it is important to identify possible meanings of "responsibility." The first of these deals only with *the production of effects*, not with the reasons for action or the circumstances in which action occurs. You are responsible for what you cause, in the local causality, low foreseeability, no coercion sense of causality. Since behavior does engulf the field, obscuring essential aspects of the environment, this category can cover a lot of ground.

2. A second sense of responsibility, overlapping somewhat with the first, is *legal accountability.* And since the law is designed to protect as well as to punish, it is almost impossible to characterize this sense of the word in any clear conceptual terms. It cannot be limited to actions that you produce, since you are not responsible for some that you do produce (the insanity defense) and at the same time are responsible for some that you do not locally cause (legal responsibility of parents for the actions of their children). Worse, legal accountability sometimes is determined more by the degree of consequences than by their nature. For instance, in most states it becomes necessary to determine legal responsibility for an automobile accident not whenever one occurs, but only when the damage exceeds a certain dollar amount.

3. Finally, as if the confusion between production of action and legal accountability were not enough, responsibility can also refer to *moral culpability* (blameworthiness) or *moral laudability* (praiseworthiness). This sense of the word is perhaps the least well defined of all. Production of action is observable. The actions for which you can be held legally accountable may be conceptually inconsistent, but they are usually well specified in the law. Moral culpability or laudability, however, is a value judgment made by the perceiver that may or may not be entirely consistent with the behavioral evidence. For example, in the later years of American involvement in the Vietnam war, when the official policy of the United States was withdrawal, there were still "hawks" in Congress who considered peace demonstrators to be "responsible" for prolonging the conflict. Were the demonstrators considered responsible in the production-of-action sense? Most probably not. Were they legally accountable? No. But were they considered blameworthy and deserving of sanctions? Most assuredly. Here, the judgment of responsibility was as much in the eye of the perceiver as in the behavior of the actor.

As final points in our discussion of causality and of responsibility, two important differences between these concepts should be noted. First, as causality is usually considered, it is relatively free of distortion based on the affective consequences of the action in question. Whether I believe that a person I observe has caused an event will depend only to a small degree on whether the consequences of the event are positive or negative. In contrast, judgments of responsibility are more likely to be heavily laden with affective or moral qualities. If a union strike closes a factory for all (even nonunion) employees, labor leaders and management may agree that the strike has *caused* temporary suspension of everyone's pay but may disagree quite strenuously on the issue of the union's *responsibility* (in the blameworthiness sense, for example) for the closing. This does not mean that judgments of causality are entirely free of consequence effects, only that those judgments are less influenced than are attributions of responsibility.

The second major difference between the two ideas is the degree of overlap among possible characterizations. First consider the meanings of causality. Once an agent has been characterized as coerced by the environment, it makes no sense to say that he was *not* a local cause. Similarly, if perceivers agree that the effects of an action were not foreseeable, it makes no sense to describe the behavior that produced those effects as intentional causality. Knowledge of one causal description can logically preclude other descriptions. With responsibility, however, the various senses of the term can apply singly or in any combination, and knowing that a person is responsible in one sense may or may not be informative about his responsibility in other senses. Indeed, you can be both morally culpable and legally accountable for an action you might even have tried to *prevent* (the friend of a burglar who tried to stop a caper becomes an accessory after the fact for not turning in his friend). Because of the differences between causality and responsibility, the remainder of the chapter will consider them as separate issues, risking artificiality in hope of gaining clarity of exposition.

Causality

As the discussions of the three attribution theories suggest, Kelley's theory is most appropriate for the subject of causality. Heider's model is more relevant to responsibility assignment than to causality; the correspondent inference theory of Jones and Davis is more directed toward dispositional attributions from actions in cases in which causality is not typically in question. Certainly these other theories contain material relevant to causality, and it will be mentioned when appropriate. Most of the discussion will, however, be based on Kelley's more comprehensive treatment of causality (see, for example, 1971, 1972, and 1973). In brief, this approach suggests the ways in which attributors might distinguish among the multiple possible causes of events on the basis of a principle of *covariation.*

The idea that there are multiple possible causes for behavioral events was introduced in Heider's (1958) conception that both personal and environmental forces contribute to action. Most frequently, his environmental force (e.g., task difficulty) takes the form of what Kelley (1971) calls an *inhibitory cause,* since it represents a barrier to action that must be overcome by personal force. There are cases, however, in which Heider uses environmental force (now opportunity or luck) as what Kelley (1971) calls a *facilitative cause,* which increases the likelihood of successful action. The idea of multiple possible causes is also recognized by Jones and Davis (1965) when they show that in-role behavior is less dispositionally informative than is out-of-role behavior. When an actor has role requirements as well as his own dispositions directing his actions, a perceiver cannot be certain which contributes more heavily to the action. Finally, Bem's self-perception theory (Chapter 6) is based on the fact that individuals may have difficulty distinguishing between the internal and external possible causes of even their own behavior.

What Kelley has done is to specify with more precision how a perceiver might distinguish among various multiple possible causes. The first way in which this was accomplished was by partitioning of environmental forces into those connected with the entity and those connected with the situation (Chapter 4). One of the benefits to be realized from this partition is a better explanation of apparently unique occurrences (luck). As research by McArthur (1972) indicates, when perceivers are asked to attribute causality to person, entity, or situation (singly or in combination) for data patterns of low consistency over time and persons, with high distinctiveness among entities, the preponderant choice is "situation." In other words, when a person who ordinarily does not like movies is enthralled by a film that nobody else likes (and that even he does not like when he sees it a second time), it is intuitively more satisfying to attribute this reaction to transient features of the particular situation than to either an enduring personal disposition or to an unchanging aspect of the entity. By accounting for instances of luck in this manner, the person-entity-situation partition represents an improvement over earlier person-environment notions.

A second increase in precision of causal attribution is provided by Kelley's (1971) more thorough conceptualization of multiple possible causes. For example, if you say as Heider might, that a personal attribution will be high if there is a high task difficulty overcome, you are making a single specific assertion. If, however, you abstract from this statement the principle that an internal facilitative cause will be seen as stronger when it successfully overcomes an external inhibitory cause, you have significantly increased the power of your explanation. You have identified two sorts of causes, facilitative and inhibitory, and have implied that both sorts of causes may be found in the person or in the environment, or both. At the concrete level of "task difficulty" it would not be helpful to speak of "task difficulty within the person," but at the abstract level of the causal principle, it is easy to conceive of an internal facilitative cause (desire for a promotion) overcoming an internal inhibitory cause (restraint against being immodest).

In addition to the facilitative-inhibitory and internal-external dimensions of multiple possible causes, Kelley suggests two basic ways in which these causes may be combined. *Multiple necessary causes* must all be present if the effect for which they are necessary is to occur. This data pattern is illustrated in Figure 7-1*A*, which shows that if either of two multiple necessary causes is absent, the effect (E) will not occur. The other portion of the figure, *B*, illustrates a data pattern for the production of an effect through *multiple sufficient causes*. The effect shown (E) occurs when either of these facilitative causes is strong, or when both are present in moderate strength, but does not occur when both causes are weak. These patterns of interaction of multiple causes can be generalized, as Kelley (1972) points out, to more complex situations in which there are nonadditive as well as additive combinations, or in which a necessary cause at one level of analysis can be considered a multiple sufficient cause at another level.

What of the perceiver's attribution? In the case of multiple necessary causes, the perceiver can be certain that all necessary causes were present, but in the case of multiple sufficient causes such certainty cannot always be achieved. Suppose I succeed in rowing a boat across a river. At a first level of analysis you might perceive that

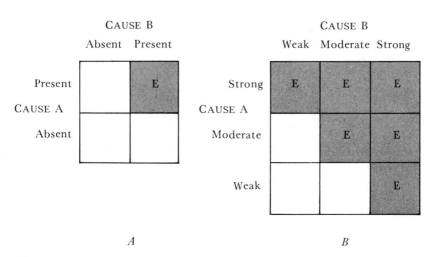

Figure 7-1. Multiple necessary (*A*) and multiple sufficient (*B*) causes. (After Kelley, 1972.)

three multiple necessary causes were present: a boat, an intention to row across the river, and the requisite ability to carry out that intention. But now the analysis becomes slightly more difficult. Presence or absence of the boat is a single cause, as is presence or absence of the intention to row across the river, and both are necessary. In contrast, "requisite ability" is itself a state resulting from the combination of multiple sufficient causes. I may have such great ability that I could perform the action regardless of the environmental inhibitory causes (current, wind) acting against me, or I may have so little ability that I could not perform the action without the assistance of environmental facilitative causes (again, these could be current and wind) acting in concert with me. In the case of such multiple sufficient causes, Kelley argues that the perceiver will employ a *discounting principle:* a given possible cause will be discounted as the sole source of given effect if there are other possible sufficient causes also present. If the wind and the current are with me as I row across the river, my ability will be discounted as the sole cause of success. In passing, it should be noted that this discounting principle is for causality attribution the equivalent of the Jones and Davis correspondent inference notion for dispositional attributions (1965). Correspondence, you will remember, increases as the noncommon effects (multiple sufficient causes) decrease, and the assumed desirability (causal strength) of alternatives to the dispositional attribution also decreases.

Given the discounting effect, how can a perceiver ever achieve any degree of assurance of the correctness of an attribution when there are multiple sufficient causes? The answer to this question lies in the fundamental principle of *covariation.* Just as the scientist might vary stimulus conditions to observe when an effect appears and disappears, Kelley argues that the attributor systematically varies entities, situations, and other persons to observe when the effect in question does and does not occur. If anyone, no matter how weak, can row across the river, the external facilitative causes of wind and current assume greater importance than the internal facilitative cause of ability. If only *I* can accomplish the task repeatedly, then my ability grows in attributional importance. With each successive variation of the situation, provided the same effect occurs, the perceiver becomes a little more confident that he knows which of the multiple possible causes is producing the effect. The perceiver, like the scientist, can never be absolutely certain that he is correct (and it only takes one failure to destroy the hypothesis entirely). Through successive observations (or obtaining information from several independent sources at the same time), however, greater certainty in causal attribution can be achieved.

Effects can have single or multiple causes, and attributors can obtain information about causality through repeated observation of the covariations between effects and potential causes. When an effect has a single cause, the perceiver's task is a simple one: presence of the effect necessarily implies presence of the cause, so temporal contiguity is the only attributional clue required. In a similar way, if an effect is the product of multiple necessary causes, occurrence of the effect indicates that all of these were present. The final attribution will be less clear when the effect has multiple *sufficient* causes. Each of these will be discounted as the explanation for the effect in direct proportion to the number of alternatives. Certainty about which of several multiple sufficient causes is most influential can only be approached, never completely attained, and only through repeated observation of variations across situations, persons, and entities. All causes, whether single or multiple, can be classified as internal within the actor or as external to him; as facilitative or inhibitory of the effect in question.

Summary

Responsibility

MORE ON THE MEANING OF RESPONSIBILITY

As noted in the beginning of this chapter, the term *responsibility* can have at least three different meanings: causality, legal accountability, and moral accountability. Before considering some of the factors that can affect attributions of responsibility, we should try to determine which of the three meanings best approximates the attribution that actually is made. Although attribution theorists and researchers alike have not been too careful in specifying which meaning is intended, some consistent patterns of usage can be found.

Most theoretical statements do not appear to be limited to the causality sense of the term. For example, the first social-psychological study of responsibility was the work of Fauconnet (1920), who examined uses of the term in European and Asian social practices and penal codes. Although he identified five different categories of usage, Fauconnet did conclude that "responsibility is born outside of the responsible person. It comes upon him because he finds himself in circumstances that engender it" (1920, p. 91). Social necessity, as well as causality, is involved. The suggestion that attributions of responsibility include more than simple causality also finds support in Piaget's study of moral development in children (1932). Piaget distinguished between an "objective" responsibility employed by very young children, in which the degree of moral accountability depends only on amount of damage, not on intention or circumstances, and a "subjective" conception developed later which takes motives into account. Both of these conceptions hinge on factors other than mere causality.

Turning to the major attribution theorists, Heider (1944, 1958) extended Fauconnet's analysis and argued that the perceiver's personal needs, as well as more general social necessity, might influence attributions of responsibility. A person may be thought of as the prototype of an origin in part because he is a readily identifiable target for the application of sanctions. You cannot take restitution from, or revenge against, a situation. In discussing the implications of correspondent inference theory, Jones and Davis (1965) do not directly concern themselves with attributions of responsibility. The dispositional attributions they mention, however, assume that the stimulus person is responsible for his actions, and these dispositional attributions can be affected by hedonic relevance and personalism. Again there is the implication that the perceiver's needs might influence the attribution of responsibility. Finally, although Kelley's (1967) preference is for cognitive, rather than motivational, interpretations of attributional phenomena, he does cite cases in which responsibility is determined by factors other than pure causality.

Not only does the attribution of responsibility seem to involve more than a simple judgment of causality, the descriptive language used by theorists and the potential for motivational influences on perceivers suggest that the attributional product is more of a moral assertion than a legal one. Fauconnet speaks of assigning sanctions to the person, Piaget uses "naughtiness" almost interchangeably with "responsibility" when eliciting attributions from his children, and Heider writes of sanctions and blame. Social necessity and the perceiver's needs should be much less important in determining legal accountability than in establishing moral accountability. No matter how much I may want to believe that a stimulus person is morally corrupt, my level of motivation will not alter the way in which effects are produced by him (leading to a judgment of causality where none exists) or the way laws are written (leading to a judgment of illegality when no laws have been violated). It can, however, cause me to see him as *morally* responsible for evil. To his pleas for reasonableness in judgment I might reply, "Of course I know that you did not personally violate any laws, or personally cause any evil effects, but just the same you are *responsible*." Motivation can certainly lead to exaggerations of causality and legal accountability, but these cannot easily be maintained in the face of contradictory evidence. Beliefs in moral culpability or laudability, on the other hand, can serve personal needs to such a degree that objective reality may never sway them. It is probably fair to conclude, then, that "responsibility" as used by attribution theorists refers principally to an *evaluation of moral accountability.* Whether most perceivers use the term in that sense is presently an open question.

Factors Influencing Responsibility Attribution

Attributions of responsibility can be influenced by characteristics of the actor, aspects of the situation, and the personal needs of the perceiver. Considering the actor and situation first, more responsibility will be assigned to an actor for an intentional action than for an accidental occurrence. This statement is interesting only because it is probably the strongest one that could be made about this relationship. It does not preclude the possibility of responsibility assignment for an accident (what traffic policeman will believe that an automobile accident was really *nobody's* fault?), and it does not assert that complete responsibility will be assigned for all entirely intentional actions. We perceivers are all too willing to assign responsibility for negative occurrences (even when they may involve no intention), but we are reluctant to give complete credit for a wholly intentional behavior that leads to positive outcomes. If this tendency were strong enough in a particular perceiver, he might attribute more blame for a negative outcome than credit for a positive one, even if the level of intention were identical in both cases.

Another reason that complete responsibility is not assigned on the basis of intention alone is that the actor's motivation and ability (as well as the situational factors of task difficulty, luck, and success or failure) all have bearing on the attributional decision. How many times have you watched an athlete, such as a gymnast, a diver, or a figure-skater, execute an intricate maneuver so smoothly that he "made it look easy?" Now if you didn't have any information about how difficult the task was (if you had never tried the activity yourself), you might well conclude that the task was simple. You have seen no apparent effort, and the performer does not look superhuman, so you conclude that almost anyone could successfully complete the action. Of course, you would be mistaken. The important point is that in the attribution of responsibility for success, a number of interrelated factors need to be considered. What about an attribution of responsibility for failure? Not surprisingly, a person who fails because he does not try is held more morally accountable than is a person who fails because he does not have the requisite ability (Jones and deCharms, 1957). Lack of ability is not under the actor's immediate control, and so is forgiveable, but lack of motivation, especially when coupled with what would have been sufficient ability, cannot be excused. For a more complete review of other processes involved in the attribution of responsibility for success and failure, see Weiner et al. (1971).

Perhaps the best way to summarize the participation of the actor and the situation in the production of effects is just to restate Heider's original proposition: The more the effect appears to be under the immediate personal control of the actor, the more responsibility will be assigned to him. We now know, of course, that this is an unsophisticated view. For example, is an accident to be considered at the level of Forseeability, or Causality, or somewhere in between? How is nonintentional but single causality differently represented in the "levels model" from nonintentional multiple sufficient causality? Given intentional action, how is Intentionality with a major component of motivation differently conceptualized from the same level with a major component of ability? The basic postulation of five different levels of responsibility obviously does not take these or other complex questions into account. Nevertheless, some continuing research by Shaw, Sulzer, and their associates (Shaw and Sulzer, 1964; Sulzer, 1971) indicates that the levels do embody distinctions that are meaningful to perceivers. Across a wide variety of subject populations, these studies demonstrate that when individuals are asked to evaluate sets of situations describing all of the five levels, the responsibility attributed to the actor will *increase* from Association to Causality to Foreseeability to Intentionality, and then will *decrease* to Justifiability (to approximately the Causality level).

Before concluding that all attributions of responsibility are unbiased reflections of the stimulus conditions (the relative contributions of actor and situation), we should take a closer look at the perceiver himself. When we do so, we will discover that even with the stimulus conditions constant, different perceivers will assign varying amounts of responsibility to the stimulus person. There are a number of classes of reasons why this might be the case, and three of those classes—personality differences among perceivers, variations in the perceiver's view of his task, and distortions in attribution resulting from the perceiver's motivation—have received the most attention.

There are several personality variables that might influence attributions of responsibility to others, and three of them will be mentioned here. First, the same individual differences in *locus of control* that affect self-perception will also influence responsibility attribution. As deCharms (1968) and others have shown, people who believe that most of their own outcomes depend not on external forces but on their own behavior attribute more originship to others as well. We generalize from our own circumstances, assuming that other people have about the same degree of control over their lives as we feel we have over our own.

A second possible personality influence is what Kohlberg (1969) calls level of *moral development,* and this influence may be especially important when the stimulus person and the situation are multiple sufficient causes of the effect. For example, to paraphrase one of Kohlberg's standard situations, suppose that a stimulus person desperately needs a special medicine to save his spouse's life. Because the stimulus person is not wealthy, and because the pharmacist charges one hundred times as much for the drug as it costs to produce, the only way the stimulus person can obtain any is to steal it. Is he morally accountable for doing so? Some perceivers will see this as a clear case of Intentionality, and attribute a great deal of responsibility to the actor. Others will believe that the druggist (for overcharging) and the "system" (for not providing life-saving drugs at prices anyone can afford) share enough of the blame to make this a case of Justifiability. The objective circumstances are identical, but perceivers interpret those circumstances differently.

While Kohlberg's concept of moral development deals primarily with moral accountability, more general differences in cognitive style can also lead to interpretive differences, and one such dimension, *dogmatism,* provides our third example. In an extensive analysis of this trait, Rokeach (1960) shows how dogmatic people are more likely to prefer simple answers to complex questions and are less likely to search for additional information than are their more open-minded counterparts. In terms of attribution of responsibility, we would expect highly dogmatic people to be less aware of extenuating circumstances at the same time that they would be more likely to let the behavior of the actor engulf the field and provide the sole explanation for an event's occurrence.

Not only can relatively enduring aspects of the perceiver's character affect his attributions of responsibility, his view of his task may also influence the process. For example, Jones and Thibaut (1958) have identified three general strategies (or *sets*) that a perceiver might take in perceiving another person, and these can be applied to the case of responsibility attribution. In the *causal-genetic set* the perceiver is acting like a psychologist, attempting to understand the actor's behavior without placing any value judgments on that behavior. The perceiver is detached from the situation, and his goal is to be as objective as possible. In the *situation-matching set* the perceiver is acting like a juror, evaluating the stimulus person's behavior to determine whether that behavior deserves sanctions. Because of the necessity for assignment of sanctions, the perceiver's emotional involvement is greater, although there is still an emphasis on objectivity in evaluation. Finally, in the *value-maintenance set* the perceiver is concerned with the attainment of his own goals, and this concern leads to the greatest emotional involvement and the most subjective judgment. The attributional problems that arise in this last conception of the perceiver's task can be summed up in the old adage that "a lawyer who chooses to represent himself has a fool for a client."

RESEARCH ON RESPONSIBILITY ATTRIBUTION

We have seen that the attribution of responsibility to an actor will depend in part on the relative contributions of the person and the environment, in part on the perceiver's personality traits, and in part on the cognitive set he takes when approaching the attribution task. In the beginning of this chapter we distinguished between responsibility in a production-of-action sense and responsibility in a moral accountability sense, and this distinction becomes important when we consider a final factor that may influence responsibility attribution: the *motivation* of the perceiver.

Suppose that you are asked to evaluate the personal worth of a suffering victim. Let us assume that you do not want to believe that you yourself might have to undergo such pain. If that is the case, you cannot conclude that the victim is suffering "by chance," since that would raise the possibility that similar bad luck might befall you. Under these circumstances there are only two attributionally acceptable possibilities. First, you might see the person as being responsible (in the production-of-action sense) for his own suffering: "If he had been minding his own business, he wouldn't have been hurt." This sort of attribution would permit you to comfort yourself with the knowledge that *you* would not have behaved as stupidly and therefore would not have received the same fate. Alternatively, if you were convinced that the person was not production-of-action responsible for his predicament, you might still protect yourself by asserting that the victim was morally reprehensible (the moral accountability sense of responsibility) and thus deserved what he was getting.

This assertion that the victim of suffering "deserved what he got" is an attributional strategy for self-protection that Lerner (1966) has called the *belief in a just world*. Rather than admit the possibility that negative occurrences could happen merely as a result of capricious chance (a highly threatening situation), the perceiver chooses to believe that the negative outcomes individuals receive are *deserved*, either by virtue of the recipient's behavior or by virtue of his intrinsic moral accountability. An interesting series of studies serves to illustrate this process, showing its consequences for various interpersonal judgments.

The relationship between behavior and moral accountability as explanations for suffering is most clearly demonstrated in a study by Lerner and Matthews (1967). In this experiment female subjects participated in pairs in what was described as an investigation of the effects of various reinforcements on learning. The particular reinforcements to be used were described as electric shock (negative) and money (positive). After receiving these initial instructions together, the two subjects were placed in separate waiting rooms in anticipation of being run in separate laboratories. Each woman was then told that one of them would be randomly assigned to the negative reinforcement condition, while the other would be assigned either to the positive reinforcement condition or to an innocuous control condition. So, from the subject's point of view, her own possibilities were either shock/reward or shock/control.

These condition assignments were to be accomplished by having each member of the pair of subjects pick a slip from a bowl, and the *number* of slips actually present in the bowl was varied to produce differences in the degree to which the fates of the two subjects were interdependent. At one extreme, the Fates Interdependent condition, there were only two slips present in the bowl, one ostensibly having the word "shock" written on it, the other having either the word "control" or the word "reward" written on it. It was made clear to the subjects in this Fates Interdependent condition that whichever subject chose her slip *first* would in effect be assigning *both* subjects to their respective conditions. The actual choice of condition assigment slips was performed after the subjects were separated, and in fact one slip contained the word "control," one the word "reward." No slips ever contained the word "shock."

Now, imagine that you are a subject in this experiment. You know that your fate is intertwined with the other subject's, and you are waiting alone to receive the condition assignment. The experimenter arrives with two slips in the bowl and asks you to choose one. You do, and it says "reward" or "control." You believe that the other slip says "shock," so you know that you are *responsible,* in the production-of-action sense, both for your own good fortune and for the other's bad fortune. She is, in an important way, an innocent victim of your choice and will suffer through no behavioral fault of her own. After you have made your choice you are asked to evaluate the other subject's attractiveness on a number of rating scales. How do you evaluate the innocent victim? You decide that she is *unattractive,* implying (as Lerner argues) that she deserves to suffer by virtue of being a bad person.

With only two condition assignment slips in the bowl, there is another possibility. You are waiting in your room to receive your condition assignment, and the experimenter appears with the bowl, now containing a single slip. You draw it, and it says "reward" or "control." As the experimenter explains, the other subject picked her slip first, assigning herself to the shock condition and assigning you to either the reward or control condition. In our terms, now the other subject is production-of-action responsible for her own bad fortune (and for your good fortune). In this case your evaluation of her is *positive:* there is no need to derogate a person who can be seen as behaviorally responsible for her own suffering.

In the other condition, called Fates Independent, each waiting subject was asked to choose her condition assignment by drawing a slip from a bowl that contained a very large number of slips. Again, the bowl contained only "reward" and "control" slips, although the experimenter stated that it contained "shock" slips as well. After you have drawn your "reward" or "control" slip, the experimenter casually remarks that the other subject had drawn a "shock" slip. You are production-of-action responsible for your own fate, and she is production-of-action responsible for hers. In this case, your evaluations of the other subject are relatively objective—no enhancement of her attractiveness, but no real derogation either. The session was terminated after the evaluations were completed—the purported learning experiment never actually took place.

This study illustrates the extent to which a perceiver's need to believe in a just world may distort his evaluations of an innocent victim. When an attribution of responsibility (production-of-action sense) is made impossible by the situation, an attribution of moral accountability will be made in order to justify suffering. This process has a number of important social implications. For example, consider the response of a person who believes that the reason welfare recipients are such a drain on the national, state, and local treasuries is that "they don't want to work." In other words, they are personally responsible (in a sort of failure-to-produce-action sense) for their unfortunate condition. What may happen if well-meaning social scientists can convince this person that the welfare recipients are "on the rolls" through no fault of their own, that in fact they are innocent victims of the technocracy? The person may change his views, but in a way we might not desire. If there is a need to believe in a just world, he may decide that welfare recipients are in the position they are in because they are simply bad people. Their plight is an appropriate punishment for being morally reprehensible.

In much the same way that the need to believe in a just world may distort attributions made to an innocent victim, other self-protective tendencies may bias the attributions made to potential perpetrators of negative occurrences. In the first study of this sort, Walster (1966) asked subjects to evaluate the responsibility of a person whose parked and empty automobile rolled down a hill. The consequences of this accident were described either as being inconsequential or quite serious, depending in part on how far down the hill the car rolled before stopping and on the presence or absence of people at the bottom of the hill. In the least serious condition the car stopped after rolling just a few feet, because of a stump that was protruding into the street. Here the only damage was to the car—a slight dent in the fender. In contrast, the most serious outcome occurred when the automobile rolled all the way down the hill and crashed into a small grocery store, totally demolishing the car and injuring the grocer and a boy who happened to be standing at the counter.

What are the attributional possibilities? Recall that an accident is supposed to be attributionally valueless by definition. In theory the only attributionally meaningful actions are *intentional* actions, and accidents are, by definition, not intended. Now if the perceiver were a totally rational processor of information, he would most probably attribute the unfortunate occurrence to chance, and his attribution would not differ depending upon the severity of the consequences of the accident. But is the perceiver wholly rational about the matter? Walster suggests that he is not. To attribute an accident to chance would imply that a similar misfortune could befall anyone (obviously including the perceiver). This might be no problem in the case of a minor accident, but what perceiver would like to think that he could suffer a catastrophe? Walster argued that while the perceiver could accept the occurrence of a minor accident, he would have to attribute responsibility for the severe occurrence to the automobile's owner, comforting himself with the belief that in the same circumstances *he* would have acted differently (and would thus have prevented the occurrence).

As predicted, the results showed that more responsibility was attributed to the car's owner when the accident was serious than when it was minor (it must be assumed that this is really moral accountability, rather than production-of-action, since the driver was not even near the car at the time). Unfortunately, a surprisingly large number of other studies have failed to replicate this overall difference in attributions of responsibility for accidents with differing severity of consequences.

One series of failures to replicate the attributional differences that Walster found for mild and severe accidents led Shaver (1970) to conclude that there were at least two factors involved in the perceiver's attribution. First, for any degree of threat to be aroused

[margin annotation:] refutation of information processing

[margin annotation:] w/ possible motive to prevent another accident.

there must be *situational possibility*—the perceiver must think that it is possible that he might find himself in circumstances similar to those surrounding the stimulus person. You probably drive a car, you occasionally park it on hills, so situational possibility should make such an accident threatening to you. What is your first attributional response? Attribute responsibility to the car's owner and convince yourself that "if I had been in his shoes, *I* would have been much more careful." You have successfully avoided having to attribute the accident to "chance," and you have convinced yourself that you would avoid the accident, even under the same circumstances, because you would have acted differently. What if I told you that I know you and the stimulus person very well, and I can see a great deal of *personal similarity* between the two of you? In other words, I am implying that if you were to find yourself in the situation, the chances are good that you *would* make the same mistakes. Now if you were to say that the stimulus person was responsible (remember that this is most probably in the moral accountability sense), you are setting harsh standards by which your own future conduct might be judged. It would be bad enough for you to be involved in an accident, and even worse for everyone to blame you for its occurrence. If this is the alternative, then in this particular case an attribution to "chance" might be preferable.

This entire chain of inferences follows a strategy that Shaver (1970) calls *defensive attribution:* a desire on the part of perceivers to make whatever attributions will best reduce the threat posed by the situation. If you are faced with a threatening attributional situation, in which threat can be reduced by attributing responsibility and denying personal similarity, you will do that. If you cannot deny personal similarity, then you are more likely to attribute the negative outcome to chance. This defensive attribution notion has received support in a number of studies (e.g., Chaikin and Darley, 1973; Shaver, Turnbull, and Sterling, 1973) and may provide an alternative to the view of a perceiver who is maintaining a belief in a just world. For example, what happens if the innocent victim (who according to the just world should be devalued) happens to be *you.* Are you really likely to assert that you deserved to suffer because of your bad moral character? It is more probable that under these circumstances you will defensively relinquish your belief in a just world, arguing that there are at least a few cases in which negative outcomes are the result of bad luck. Whichever formulation eventually has the most explanatory value, the essential point remains: a perceiver's own self-protective motivation can sometimes distort his attributions of responsibility.

Of all the attributions that a perceiver can make, causality and responsibility are the most fundamental, since further attributions of dispositional properties, at least in principle, require a belief that the actor has intentionally produced the effects of interest. Causality can be internal to the actor, external to him, or jointly determined. In the case of multiple sufficient causes of action, the perceiver will discount any single one in proportion to the number of other alternatives present; estimates of the actual source will improve with repeated observation of the cause-effect covariations. Responsibility can mean legal accountability, moral accountability, or production-of-action; depending upon the particular meaning it can at times be equivalent to causality, at times more than causality, and at times less than causality. The attributions of responsibility made by perceivers can reflect accurately the objective content of the situation, or they can be distorted by the perceiver's personal needs. The task for future research is to identify the limiting conditions that determine which of these possibilities will occur. We now turn to the next step in the attributional chain, the inference of dispositional properties within the actor.

8

ATTRIBUTIONS TO OTHERS:
PERSONAL DISPOSITIONS

We began this book with what seemed at the time to be a simple proposition: People search for meaning in human behavior. In the course of showing how that search might proceed, we have discovered the full dimensions of the problem. Let's examine the proposition more closely. Who are the people doing the searching? They could be described as experienced perceivers who, because of their intelligence and empathic ability, make generally accurate categorizations of other people. Less charitably, they might also be described as self-seeking distorters of reality who are sometimes so confused that they do not know even what they themselves feel until they see what they do. What about the object of their attention? The stimulus person is not merely a collection of attributes, he is a thinking being engaged in active self-presentation. And not all of his behavior is attributionally interesting, since habits and accidents are not considered reflections of underlying dispositional properties. Apparently both the stimulus and the perceiver are substantially more complicated than it would appear at first glance.

How does the search for meaning proceed? Certainly it involves observation of action, judgment of intention, and dispositional attribution. But some dispositional attributions are made without prior judgment of intention, and some obviously intentional actions do not lead to dispositional attribution. Finally, what meaning is discovered? Presumably, the informed perceiver will have a satisfactory explanation for the behavior of interest and will be better able to predict its likelihood of occurrence in the future. But both of these outcomes can be complicated by role requirements, by other actions that would have been possible, and by the perceiver's own motivation. The process, like the people performing it, is more complex than it first appears. In this chapter we will reexamine the concept of dispositional attribution, using what we have learned along the way to suggest more completely what the process may, or may not, involve.

More on Observation of Action with an Example from Attribution of Ability

Throughout the preceding chapters we have shown how the would-be attributor is an active perceiver who contributes something of his own to the attributions that he makes. The perceiver's contribution is, of course, most apparent when the information he receives is ambiguous and he has an important stake in the attribution to be made. The athlete doing his own refereeing, the man-about-town evaluating his date, and the observer of a suffering victim are all examples containing this potential for bias. But there are other instances of attributional errors that can be based on factors as divorced from motivation as the organization of the behavioral data. This possibility is illustrated in a set of experiments reported by Jones, Rock, Shaver, Goethals, and Ward (1968).

Just as Asch (1946) found order effects in the presentation of descriptive adjectives, Jones and his colleagues discovered that when an attribution is based on bits of behavior, those elements early in the series can take primacy over the ones that come later. Their subjects watched a film of a stimulus person attempting to solve a series of analogies and progressions ostensibly drawn from a standardized test "designed to discriminate at the highest levels of intelligence."

There were three experimental conditions. In the first of these the stimulus person's correct answers formed a descending pattern —seven out of the first eight items correct, followed by a gradual decline in performance through the series. The second condition was a mirror image of the first, with the stimulus person's apparent performance ascending from a poor start to a flying finish. In the third condition the apparently correct items were scattered randomly through the series, but in all three conditions the number of correct answers was the same: 15 out of the 30 possible. The results showed that not only did the subjects predict higher performance for the descending pattern, they also judged that stimulus person to be more intelligent.

After ruling out some possible alternative explanations of the results, Jones and his co-workers concluded that these primacy effects were most probably due to an *expectancy* established by the early trials. Ability is a dispositional property that should remain relatively constant over time, so performance differences on an intellectual task should reflect variations in motivation, rather than ability. Now if motivation is also assumed to be constant (and there was no reason to believe otherwise), the stimulus person's successes should be just as evenly distributed. The perceivers would then expect that the level of performance shown on the first several trials would continue throughout the series, and it should provide a good estimate of the stimulus person's ability. In fact, when asked to recall the absolute number of correct items, perceivers consistently overestimated the number correct in the descending condition. Whether or not further research supports this cognitive explanation of the findings, the important point for our purposes is that, when the disposition concerned is presumed to be a stable one, a perceiver who observes bits of behavior may exhibit a primacy effect in attribution. In other words, if you can possibly avoid being a "late-bloomer" you had better do so, since attributions can be affected by the primacy effect and other factors of stimulus organization.

More on the Role of Intention with an Example from Attribution of Attitudes

As first noted in Chapter 3, there are three basic elements of the attribution process: observation of action, judgment of intention, and dispositional attribution. We have seen how the manner in which an action is observed can affect the final dispositional attribution, and now we reconsider the second element in the chain. In Chapter 3 we argued that a true dispositional attribution requires a prior judgment of intention. Involuntary or reflex actions do not reveal dispositions, and habitual behavior serves only to establish the existence of the habit, not the dispositional properties that might have led to the habit. In a similar manner, accidental occurrences may suggest that the actor is accident-prone, but effects produced by accident should not be taken as evidence of underlying dispositions.

The importance of prior judgments of intention as preconditions for attributions was further illustrated in Chapter 5, where comparisons were made of the three attribution theories. At that time we discussed Heider's formulation, which suggests that intention is a necessary but not sufficient element of dispositional attribution. In addition to intention, Heider argued that exertion—in a degree and direction appropriate to accomplish the intention—and an absence of environmental coercion are required for dispositional attribution. In Jones and Davis's correspondent inference theory, intention is

Attributions to Others: Personal Dispositions **115**

again a necessary, but not sufficient component of dispositional attribution. There must also be an absence of external influence, not only from the iron fist of coercion but also from the velvet glove of high desirability. Finally, Kelley's attribution theory agrees that intention is necessary but suggests, somewhat surprisingly, that it is also sufficient for dispositional attribution. This sufficiency is accomplished by redefining the concept of intention to exclude all behavior for which there is a possible external contributory cause. For example, a banker who laboriously opens a complicated combination lock on his safe is *not* considered to have performed an intentional behavior if there is a gunman holding a pistol to his head. Thus, although there are differences in usage, all three theories do agree that dispositional attributions should depend on prior judgments of intention.

There are, however, several important exceptions to this general rule. Perhaps the most dramatic of these exceptions comes from the self-perception research discussed in Chapter 6. The student who believes himself to be more attracted to a nude, or less repelled by a snake, just on the basis of a presumed change in his heart rate is making an important dispositional attribution to himself. This attribution is made not only in the absence of intentional action on his part, but also in response to an apparent physiological change over which he has no intentional control. In fact, the therapeutic value of the cognitive misattribution technique depends on the possibility of producing convincing dispositional attribution in the absence of intentional action.

A second class of exception to the necessity for prior judgment of intention consists of the attributions of responsibility sometimes made for accidental occurrences. Here the question of intentionality is excluded by definition: an accident is an event that is not intentionally produced. Within this class of attributions it is important to distinguish among the various senses of the word *responsibility*. An attribution of causality, or even of legal accountability, is not usually the sort of thing we mean when we speak of a dispositional attribution. Causality and legal accountability are determined in specific situations, and only if such situations are repeated often are there any implications for the stimulus person's underlying character. For example, judgments that an individual is accident-prone or beliefs that a criminal has become "hardened" beyond any hope of rehabilitation are based on repeated instances of behavior, and at the same time it is widely recognized that even careful and conscientious people can have occasional accidents.

Consequently, only the morally accountable sense of responsibility typically qualifies as a true dispositional attribution. Even with this restriction of the possibilities, there are still numerous cases in which dispositional attributions of responsibility are made on the basis of accidental occurrences. This is especially true when the incident is particularly threatening to the perceiver. For example, the strong tendency to believe that victims of rape somehow "asked for it" can tell us as much about the perceiver's motivation as it does about the circumstances of the crime. Despite his attribution, not even the self-protecting perceiver will be ready to assert that the stimulus person actually *intended* to bring herself harm. Again a dispositional attribution has been made in the absence of a prior judgment of intention.

Finally, there can be dispositional attribution when the information about intention is imperfect rather than totally absent. In these cases, the attribution may be based not so much on the intentional actions of the stimulus person as on his failures to act when a clear choice was available. Perhaps best considered as a variation on the theme of behavior engulfing the field, this class can be illustrated by a series of studies reported by Jones and Harris (1967). In three separate experiments, their subjects were asked to evaluate a communicator who gave a speech either favoring or opposing Cuba's premier Fidel Castro. Before they heard the speech, the subjects were told that the speaker either had freely chosen which speech to give or had been directed by an external agent to give one speech or the other.

Although the No Choice–Choice manipulation did produce large differences in the underlying attitude attributed to the speaker, what is more interesting to us is that even in the No Choice conditions, attitudes consistent with the speech were attributed to the speaker. Even though the subjects did seem to be aware of the constraints on the speaker, they still thought that his private attitudes generally agreed with the public statement that he had made. One plausible explanation of these results can be couched in terms that are similar to those of Bem's self-perception theory (Chapter 6). What would the speaker's private attitudes have had to be in order to keep him from refusing to give the speech? The environmental pressures to comply were reasonably strong, but they were not of a life-and-death sort, so a person who found the speech unacceptable could have refused to give it. Particularly at a time when civil rights workers were openly defying what they considered to be discriminatory laws (and were getting arrested for their trouble), the failure to refuse to give a speech could have been interpreted as a passive acceptance of the position to be advocated.

As these exceptions to the rule of prior judgment of intention indicate, there can be dispositional attribution without a belief that the stimulus person acted intentionally. Some of these attributions can be based on behaviors over which intentional control is not feasible, others can be founded on actions thought to be possible but which were not taken, and still others can be primarily the result of the perceiver's motivation. You will notice that there is a common element in all of these exceptions. In an important sense, all represent *errors* in the attribution process. The cognitive misattribution of emotional arousal is an experimentally induced error created by the experimenter or therapist. Those instances in which behavior engulfs the field, obscuring relevant environmental constraints, are errors that any perceiver might make given the same situation. And finally, defensive attribution of responsibility is an error based on the individual's personal needs. Since all of the exceptions to the rule do lead to attributional errors, the proposition introduced in Chapter 3 can be restated as follows: Dispositional attributions can sometimes be made without prior judgment of intention, but only intentional actions can lead to veridical dispositional attribution. It is important to notice that in a few cases veridical attribution is not desirable. As we shall see in Chapter 9, it may be "better" for a phobic to misattribute his fear to an emotionally irrelevant stimulus than to be constantly afraid of objects with which he is always in contact. This is true even though a misattribution cure is still technically based on an attributional error.

More on the Nature of a Disposition with an Example from Attribution of Personality Traits

Having looked more closely at the process of dispositional attribution, we now turn to the outcome of that process and discover that it, too, must be qualified. In his search for meaning in human behavior, the perceiver first asks the question "What was the cause of that event?" And, depending upon his assessment of the relative contributions of personal and environmental facilitative and inhibitory causes, he may conclude that the stimulus person was the local cause. If that is the case, then the perceiver will wonder, "Why did he do that?" This is, of course, a two-part question, involving the judgment of intention and the subsequent dispositional attribution. If the stimulus person is thought to have acted intentionally, the perceiver's certainty about the dispositional attribution will increase as the role requirements thought to be producing the actor's behavior decrease.

This latter proposition is nicely illustrated in a study by Jones, Davis, and Gergen (1961). In this experiment, subjects were asked to form an impression of a stimulus person who was participating in a fictitious job interview. Although the subjects knew that the stimulus person had been asked to play a role in the interview, they did not know that the entire situation had been written especially for the experiment. At the beginning of the tape-recorded interview, the interviewer could be heard telling the stimulus person to try to appear as eager as possible for the job—to conform to the role requirements. Half of the subjects heard the job described as that of an astronaut, a position for which the most desirable personality characteristics included inner strength and little need for other people (inner-directed). The other half of the subjects heard the job described as that of a submariner, a position for which the most desirable personality characteristics included cooperativeness, obedience, friendliness, and gregariousness (other-directed).

After the description of the job's requirements, the tape continued with a series of statements by the interviewee (the stimulus person). These statements were varied, so that the stimulus person's responses appeared either to be consistent with the role requirements or inconsistent with those requirements. Any single subject only heard one job description and one set of interviewee responses, and at the conclusion of the tape each subject was asked to guess what the interviewee "is *really* like as a person." The results were as predicted: when the stimulus person's answers were consistent with the job role requirements (the inner-directed astronaut and the other-directed submariner), he was rated as moderately independent and moderately affiliative, and the perceivers expressed little confidence in these ratings. In contrast, when the stimulus person's answers were *inconsistent* with the role requirements (the inner-directed submariner and the other-directed astronaut), the subjects' ratings were much more extreme, and they expressed high confidence in their ratings. When a person behaves in a manner opposite that dictated by the role requirements, we can be fairly certain that his behavior reflects his underlying personality.

This dispositional attribution is at once an explanation of the stimulus person's behavior and an estimate of the likelihood that he will behave in a similar manner in the future. But is a dispositional attribution, especially one about which we are certain, ever more than an explanation and prediction? Specifically, do perceivers generally treat dispositions as *causes* (the problem of the category mistake), and do they believe that dispositions are interrelated as elements of the stimulus person's unique *personality*? It is these questions that require some further discussion.

When the problem of the category mistake (Ryle, 1949) was introduced in Chapter 5, it was illustrated by an example dealing with mental disorder that may be summarized here. A person who has been confined to a mental hospital and then released is most usually thought of as an *ex-mental patient.* The disposition that is taken to be the *cause* of his confinement (the mental disorder that produced his bizarre behavior) is still thought to be present, lurking just below the surface and ready to return to activity at any moment. Worse, any subsequent aberrant action by the person will be attributed to a resurgence of the disorder, even though similar behavior in another person would be excused as a harmless eccentricity.

Unfortunately, this tendency to endow dispositions with causal force seems to be widespread, both among attribution theorists and among perceivers. For example, in Heider's formulation the source of personal force is, ultimately, the set of underlying dispositions of the actor. In much the same way, Jones and Davis argue that the actor's behavioral intentions of the moment can be traced to more stable dispositional properties of the person that do not vary across situations. Kelley is even more explicit, since his attribution theory often refers to internal states as "causes" of behavior.

For their part, perceivers seem to treat dispositions as causal; they also appear to believe that these dispositions are organized into coherent packages, which together make up the stimulus person's *personality.* To recall some earlier examples (e.g., in Chapter 2), suppose that I tell you that a certain person is "warm and friendly" and then ask you to describe the person to me in more detail. In the language of personality theory I have given you one *trait* and have asked you to list some other traits that should go with it. Now if you as a perceiver did not believe that certain traits were interrelated, you would throw up your hands in despair. Why would I be so stupid as to ask you a question that is obviously impossible to answer? But what really happens? You may respond by saying that people are different, that you feel uncomfortable making a snap judgment about people, but if I insist, you will most probably do what I ask. It is unlikely that you will adamantly refuse to answer on the ground that the question is impossible. As it turns out, you do have what Cronbach (1955) has called an *implicit personality theory,* an intuitive notion of which traits are likely to go together.

Furthermore, people apparently share some common elements of implicit personality theories. If I asked some of your friends to give a more detailed description of the "warm and friendly" person, they would give me roughly the same answers that you did. Indeed, implicit personality theories seem to be relatively consistent across different stimulus persons and levels of acquaintance, as well as across different perceivers. An interesting study by Passini and Norman (1966) illustrates the depth of this consistency. They used a method known as *peer-nomination ratings* in order to compare their results with those of earlier research. In this procedure, the perceiver is given a set of bipolar rating scales—sociable-reclusive, cooperative-negativistic, calm-anxious—and is asked to nominate a third of his group who represent one end of each scale and a third of the group who represent the other end of the scale. Since the experiment was conducted in a psychology class, each student nominated a third of the members of the class for each end of each bipolar scale. A statistical technique known as *factor analysis* (Thurstone, 1947) is then performed on the resulting trait ratings.

The factor analysis helps the researcher see which of the traits seem to cluster together, and how many different such clusters there are. For example, the analysis by Passini and Norman revealed five separable clusters (or factors), including ones such as "emotional stability," consisting of the trait scales poised-nervous, calm-anxious, and composed-excitable. In other words, the people nominated as being calm were also highly likely to be nominated as being poised and composed. This, of course, makes perfectly good sense. What is particularly interesting about Passini and Norman's findings is that they were based on trait nominations made by students who first met each other only 15 minutes before the ratings were made! Moreover, the clusters revealed through factor analysis were almost identical to clusters found in previous research (Norman, 1963) with perceivers who had known each other for as long as three years before making their judgments.

Apparently, trait ratings can tell us more about the generality of implicit personality theories among observers than they do about the actual characteristics of the stimulus persons involved. What this remarkable consistency means, as Mischel (1968) and others have pointed out, is that perceivers often overemphasize "personality" to the detriment of both the situational constraints and the stimulus person's unique characteristics. For example, suppose that you observe a stimulus person who appears composed and poised. Now let us also suppose that you are basing your judgment of him more on your implicit personality theory than on his actual behavior. You might conclude that he was also "calm" while in fact he may be so overwrought that he can barely hold himself together. The outward composure is a mask covering great anxiety, rather than a true reflection of inner peace. You may also have failed to notice that the stimulus person is confronting a person with great power over him—a situation that creates anxiety which cannot be revealed. By relying on your implicit personality theory, you have also lost sight of the possible situational influence on the person's overt behavior.

Do you make the same mistakes when evaluating your own behavior? The available evidence suggests that you probably do not. In a similar personality trait estimation study, Nisbett and Caputo (1971) asked subjects to describe some familiar and unfamiliar people (including themselves) using a bipolar trait list with an important difference. In addition to being able to describe the various stimulus persons by checking one or the other end of each scale, the subject could also respond by checking an alternative "depends on the situation." Thus, for the scale item reserved–emotionally expressive, you could describe the stimulus person (either yourself or one of the specified others) by saying that he was reserved, or that he was emotionally expressive, or that his place on the scale really depended on the situation. Interestingly enough, the results showed that while subjects routinely assigned personality traits to the various other stimulus persons, they quite frequently chose the "depends" option to describe themselves. As Jones and Nisbett (1971) point out, when the object of attention is your own action, you concentrate on the situational factors that are affecting that action, but when the object is the behavior of others, you persist in assigning causality to underlying personality characteristics. The similarity of this notion to Bem's self-perception theory should be obvious: not only do you need to see what you do to know what you think, you may also need to see what you do to know who you are! Personality dispositions with causal properties seem to be things that other people have.

In this chapter we have reviewed the concept of dispositional attribution in light of issues raised during our discussion. As a result, we have had to qualify the component analysis suggested in Chapter 3—observation of action, judgment of intention, dispositional attribution—in some important ways. We have seen that, since attribution is an interpersonal process, even the observation of behavior is subject to some of the traditional problems of person perception (the primacy effect in ability attribution is an example). In addition, we have learned that dispositional attributions can be made without prior judgments of intention, although these attributions will be in error. And finally, we have discovered that attribution theorists and perceivers (unless they are describing themselves) endow dispositions, including the collection of dispositions known as personality, with causal properties. We have examined dispositional attribution and have found the process much more complex than it first appeared. It should be emphasized that this acknowledgment of complexity does not reflect a change in the subject matter—on the contrary, it illustrates our growing sophistication in dealing with attributional problems. Now that we have acquired the conceptual tools, we may begin to ask meaningful questions about attribution processes. The final chapter offers speculations on some of these questions, and suggests how dispositional attributions, once made, can influence interpersonal behavior.

9

INTERPERSONAL AND SOCIAL CONSEQUENCES OF ATTRIBUTION

Attribution theory is founded on the presumption that people actively search for meaning in the social world around them. Another nation abruptly changes a long-standing policy toward our country, and we want to know *why*. A militant organization engages in acts of political terrorism, and we wonder what motivates them to do so. On my bachelor friend's first date with a woman, he attends to every remark she makes, looking for its meaning. We are not content merely to be passive observers of action. Whether the behavior in question is that of a nation, a group, or a single person, and whether its consequences for us are positive or negative, if that behavior is important to us, we will try to interpret it. We employ processes of attribution to *explain* action and to *predict* whether it will be repeated in the future.

In the course of this book we have discovered a great deal about the ways in which perceivers come to understand their own behavior and the behavior of other people. Although the attribution process is a complex one, it can (with some risk of oversimplification) be summarized as follows: The first element in the attribution process is the *observation of action*, broadly conceived so as to include reports of action as well as first-hand observation. Not surprisingly, the first evidence that attribution is a dynamic and social process can be seen at this stage. For example, the stimulus person (the object of an attribution) is not merely behaving, in most cases he is engaging in self-presentation, revealing to observers only what he does not mind their seeing. For his part, the perceiver is not just passively encoding all of the information available to him. He is, instead, actively constructing an impression consistent with his needs and social categories. The degree of selectivity involved in deciding *what* has happened is illustrated by the discrepancies often found in the testimony of various eyewitnesses to an incident. The courtroom setting is designed to produce the greatest possible accuracy in description, and the eyewitnesses are asked only to describe—not interpret—the incident, yet disagreements still arise.

How can you use your knowledge of the factors involved to guard against bias in your own observations of action? Since it is impossible for you to encode all the relevant information, you must first remember that your view of the situation is just that—your viewpoint. Try to take the role of the actor, to see whether he would describe the action in the same terms that you have chosen; try to put aside your expectations and prejudices, so that you can describe what did happen rather than what should have occurred; compare your description of the situation with the views of others to see if they agree with you. As a second line of defense against observational bias, try to form your impression on the basis of a complete segment of behavior. Be aware of the pervasiveness of order effects, and try to give the "late bloomers" the same consideration, based on their overall performance, that you would be tempted to give the early starters. Knowing that there are differences in viewpoint and order effects in attribution should help you to keep from being misled into thinking that your version of the situation is the "truth." Admittedly, these suggestions sound like the first chapter in a book on how to become more interpersonally sensitive, but they are thoroughly grounded in attribution theory and research.

The second element in the attribution process is the *judgment of intention*. Let us suppose that you have been a careful observer and have arrived at a relatively accurate picture of what has taken place. Now, as you begin to wonder about the possible reasons for the occurrence, you must first decide whether the action was intended. We have seen that intentional action can be distinguished from habit, reflex, or accident in several ways, and you can apply these criteria to aid in your judgment. First, since intentional actions are supposed to be goal-directed, you should be able to identify at least some objectives that the actor could plausibly have had. Your interest at this point is only to establish the *existence* of possible objectives, not to try to choose which one you think was the actor's objective. It is precisely because we cannot find plausible goals that we call some events "accidental." For example, we assume that a driver whose automobile crashes into the concrete support for an overpass has had an accident, since we cannot imagine any plausible goals that might be served by his intentionally aiming at the abutment. Should we discover that two days earlier the driver had taken out a huge life insurance policy, we immediately become suspicious. We have identified a possible objective for an intentional crash.

Existence of possible goals, though necessary, is not sufficient for a judgment of intention. As Heider (1958) points out, there are other factors involved in the determination of intention. The action must occur in the immediate vicinity of the actor (local causality), and the perceiver must believe that if the actor's present behavior were thwarted, he would choose an alternate path to the same goal (equifinality of outcome). In addition to these requirements, there is also the necessity for *exertion*. Not only must the actor be thought to have some identifiable goal, he must also appear to be trying to achieve that objective. So, in your judgment of intention, you should ask yourself whether plausible goals exist for the action, and whether the actor appears to be exerting himself in the direction of one or more of these goals. If all of the necessary conditions are present—possible goals, local causality, equifinality, and exertion —you will conclude that the action was intentionally caused.

The final step in the attribution process is the *making of a dispositional attribution*. You have observed the action and decided that it was intentionally produced, so now you are ready to try to answer the fundamental question, "Why?" As we have seen, at this point there are basically two possibilities. Either the action should be attributed to some factor in the environment (such as a characteristic of the situation or the presence of coercion), or it should be attributed to a specific underlying disposition of the actor. If you have ruled out the environment as a possible cause of an aggressive action, you don't stop with "He acted aggressively because of some [unspecified] personal disposition." You conclude that "he acted aggressively *because he is an aggressive person.*" Your choice of attribution possibilities is not between the environment in general and the person in general, but rather between a specific force in the environment and a specific personal disposition.

In making this choice you will probably employ a combination of the attributional criteria suggested by Jones and Davis (1965) and by Kelley (1967). In order to evaluate the contribution of the environment, you need to have some idea of the degree to which anyone in the same situation would respond as the actor did. If all of the effects are high in assumed desirability (or, in Kelley's terms, if there is no distinctiveness between actors in that situation) you suspect that the environment accounts for most of the action. If, on the other hand, the actor has behaved in a distinctive manner (lack of consistency among actors suggests a low assumed desirability), and if there are few noncommon effects of the action, you are in a good position to guess that the action (say, an act of aggression) should be attributed to a personal disposition of the same name ("he is an aggressive person").

As we have suggested before, this entire process of attribution seldom takes long enough for us to point to each of its components. Only in a jury setting are we likely to find ourselves taking the time to ask: "What could have been gained by that action?" "Was it intended?" "Why did he do it?" We do not often find ourselves actually speaking of things like environmental coercion, assumed desirability, or even consensus among observers unless we are called upon to defend an attribution already made. Nevertheless, a thorough specification of the possible components of an attribution may help us understand the process more fully. And we should not be misled by the time usually required for an attribution into believing that the scientific explanation of attribution is necessarily a simple one. After all, it takes calculus to explain how the batter in a baseball game is able to have his bat in the correct place when the pitch comes sailing in.

By focusing our attention upon the process of dispositional attribution, we have learned a good deal about the ways in which perceivers might come to understand both their own behavior and the actions of other people. But dispositional attribution is not a perceptual exercise performed in a social vacuum. When attributions are being shaped they are influenced by behavior and motivation; and completed attributions, in turn, help guide subsequent behavior. In the remainder of this chapter we will illustrate some of the ways in which the attributions you make might influence your own self-conception, your actions toward others, and your view of social problems. In each of these brief examples we will try to distinguish between the consequences that might follow an environmental attribution and the consequences that might follow an attribution of the same action to an underlying personal disposition.

Self-awareness

The attribution principles that we have discussed should enable you to arrive at a more accurate understanding of your own behavior. To what extent is it true that you do not know what you believe until you hear what you say? Is the amount of credit that you demand for success greater than the amount of blame you accept for failure? Can you regard yourself objectively, as another person would see you?

A recently popular technique for increasing self-awareness is the personal growth group. Whether these groups are designed to enhance awareness of sensory experience (encounter groups), to remove barriers to effective interpersonal communication (T-groups), or to identify the sources and effects of discrimination (consciousness-raising groups), they may all be characterized in attributional terms. If you should decide to join such a group, you will find that some of the time you will be a *perceiver* of the other members and some of the time you will be the *stimulus person* who is being perceived. In your role as a stimulus person, you agree to minimize self-presentation ("behave naturally"), and in your role as a perceiver, you agree to give your honest impressions of other participants. The personal and environmental attributions made under these circumstances may have substantial impact on your own self-esteem and on your impressions of other people.

Suppose that through feedback from the other persons in the group you discover that they believe you to be quite a courageous person. For years you have made environmental attributions for your courageous-appearing actions on the grounds that "the situation demanded no less." Now you discover that by virtue of their different viewpoints and experience, the others do not agree with this environmental attribution. Because they realize that many people would not behave as you have, they see your actions as *distinctive*, and make their attributions to your personal disposition. Naturally, this revelation will enhance your self-worth.

Unfortunately, veridicality in attribution is a sword that cuts both ways. After discovering the "truth" (the *consensus* of your peers), you may find that you preferred your attributional defense mechanisms. Suppose that for a long time you have held a job in which you supervise a number of other people. Further suppose that you have never been able to get along with your employees. Now you have always attributed this unpleasantness to your position (an environmental attribution). After all, who likes the boss? But in the group, where no outside statuses are permitted, you *still* find that nobody seems to care for you. It is not your position but rather your personal characteristics that people find distasteful. This sort of change from an environmental to a personal attribution can obviously be a threat to your self-esteem.

Why are the discoveries made in personal growth groups potentially so crucial to self-worth? Perhaps because of another sort of attribution, one dictated by the initial ground rules. Remember when you agreed to give, and to accept, nothing but the truth? Doing so establishes *the only possible attribution* for a statement made in the group: the person making the assertion believes it to be true. Now if someone congratulated you for being courageous *outside* the group, where truth is not the only ground rule, there could be multiple sufficient causes for the congratulatory statement. It could be flattery, it could be mistaken identity, or it could even be true. The last interpretation would, of course, be *discounted* in direct proportion to the number of other alternatives possible. Although you might like to take the statement at face value, you could not be certain that it would be correct to do so. On the other hand, when a threatening personal attribution is made outside of the group, the same discounting principle can be used to save face. It is not really that you are a bad person, only that your employee is in an angry mood, lashing out at whoever is available; or perhaps the situation has caused him to misperceive your actions. Outside the group, the uncertainty from discounting will mean that you miss an occasional compliment, but it will permit you to maintain your composure in the face of harsh criticism. Inside the group, no discounting is possible—the only available attribution is "truth"—so what is said about you will have a significantly greater effect on your self-worth.

Psychotherapy

If separating the personal attributions from the environmental ones is important in producing self-awareness under normal circumstances, it is even more vital in many kinds of psychotherapy. This is so because the avowed goal of classic psychotherapy (as opposed to some more recent behavioristic techniques) is to relieve emotional disorder by helping the client gain "insight" into the source of his anxiety. Whether this goal is achieved with extensive participation and interpretation by the therapist (as in Freudian psychoanalysis), or through a supportive atmosphere in which the client can make the discovery for himself, the outcome can be described as a more veridical attribution. After all, what is "insight" if not a correct attribution of the causes of behavior? Once this veridical attribution is achieved, the client is helped to deal directly with the real causes of his problem, rather than with the false causes erected by his defenses. It should be noted, however, that while veridical attribution can be valuable, it is not desirable for all psychotherapy (any more than it is completely desirable in self-awareness).

One significant exception involves the often highly successful therapeutic procedures collectively known as *behavior modification*. In a situation in which a classic psychotherapist might ask, "What sort of faulty psychological development might have produced these symptoms?" a behavior modifier would wonder, "What are the environmental reinforcements supporting this behavior?" The focus is not on the client's psychological history, but on the circumstances of his present environment. Behavior modification does not presume that there are deep psychodynamic influences on the client's behavior, only that the environment is providing some rewards for his symptoms. If these rewards are removed, the symptoms should disappear. There has been substantial controversy over the psychological, as opposed to the behavioral, results of such treatment. Has the client really been "cured," or will another symptom spring up to replace the one that is no longer being reinforced? Since any further consideration of this problem is well beyond the scope of our discussion, we should only note that behavior modification is an apparently successful therapeutic technique for which cognitive processes, such as attributions, are assumed to be irrelevant.

A second exception to the characterization of psychotherapy as a process designed to increase the veridicality of attribution consists of some of the newly developed misattribution therapies first mentioned in Chapter 6. As noted then, the purpose of these techniques is to derive therapeutic benefits from experimentally induced *mis*attribution of arousal to emotionally irrelevant stimuli. For example, Storms and Nisbett (1970) report partial cures of insomnia based on an induced external attribution of wakefulness. As they suggest, insomnia may be one sort of psychological problem that can be characterized as a vicious cycle: "occurrence of symptoms, worry about symptoms, consequent exacerbation of symptoms" (p. 326). Such problems should be most amenable to an attribution therapy that would externalize the cause of the symptoms. Storms and Nisbett gave some of their insomniac subjects placebo pills described as a drug capable of producing alertness, high temperature, and heart rate increases. Since all of these symptoms typically accompany insomnia, those subjects receiving the placebo could readily attribute their arousal to the pill (an external and worry-free attribution). And as anticipated, these experimental subjects reported getting to sleep earlier on nights when they took the pills than on nights when they did not. In this case an induced *mis*attribution of internally caused arousal to emotionally irrelevant external causes brought improvement. Thus, depending upon the particular psychological problem and upon the therapeutic method employed, both veridical and nonveridical separation of personal causes from environmental causes can be aids to psychotherapy.

Interpersonal Attributions and Trustworthiness

Familiarity with the principles and problems of attribution should also enhance the accuracy of your perceptions of others. If you know that the attributions of stable dispositional properties are affected by primacy, you may want to guard against possible bias by giving a closer look to the performance of "late bloomers." If you thoroughly understand how your own motivation can influence your attributional judgments, you may be more careful in forming first impressions of others, especially when the circumstances are ambiguous but important to you. If you are aware of the extent to which behavior can engulf the field, obscuring the environmental constraints on action, you may try to differentiate more carefully between the personal causes of action internal to the actor and the environmental causes also involved.

Throughout this book we have argued that you have two objectives as a perceiver: to explain actions of interest to you and to predict the likelihood of their recurrence. Now what about an actor whose behavior makes these objectives either difficult or easy to attain? We might guess that you would try to avoid a totally unpredictable actor, because some of his unpredictable actions may have bad consequences for you. But predictability alone is not enough. In our friendships, in our love affairs, and in our business dealings, we want to be involved with people we can trust. Interpersonal trust is perhaps the most fundamental characteristic of interaction—not only difficult to achieve, but easy to destroy. An attributional analysis of trustworthiness may help us to understand why this is the case.

As a beginning, we must determine that a person is acting on the basis of his "principles," rather than changing his behavior like a chameleon as the situation and persons involved vary. In terms of Kelley's model, we must observe the actor's behavior in a variety of situations with a number of different other persons present and see that it is relatively constant in order to arrive at a personal (entity) attribution for his actions. We have conducted our exercise in applied social science and have concluded that the environment can be ruled out as a cause of his behavior. Now, however, the attributional task becomes more difficult. We have succeeded in eliminating environmental causes, but we are left not with a single internal cause, but with several possible internal causes. The actions from which trustworthiness is to be inferred are most typically socially desirable. Whether these actions are conceptualized in Jones and Davis's terms as a large number of non-common highly desirable effects (concentrating on the effects produced), or in Kelley's terms as multiple sufficient facilitative causes (concentrating on the possible causes), attribution to a unique disposition of trustworthiness is obviously difficult. It is unfortunate but true that our attributions of negatively valued dispositions like hostility can be made with more certainty than attributions of positively valued dispositions, because of the great differences in assumed desirability. Since trustworthiness is only one of the possible explanations of the stimulus person's behavior, it must be discounted in proportion to the number of other alternatives. What this means for the perceiver is that there must be still more observations, under different situations, to rule out these alternatives.

Now we can begin to see why trustworthiness is such a difficult matter to establish, and why it can be so easily destroyed. The perceiver must first determine that action was based on internal principles, next that the principles are good (e.g., not manipulative) ones, and only at this point that trustworthiness is the most important principle involved. This can be a lengthy attributional process. More importantly, the perceiver's applied social science has the same limitations as formal social science—each successive confirmation makes the hypothesis of trustworthiness more tenable, but perfect certainty can never be achieved. And it takes only one counterexample to disconfirm.

Some Social Consequences of Attribution

Where does the responsibility lie for the occurrence of crime? Is it the fault of individuals who commit single acts of criminal behavior? Or should some of the blame be shared by an economic and social system that induces high expectations in all of its people, regardless of their ability to obtain promised rewards through accepted channels? What about drug abuse? Are addicts personally responsible for their fate, or have the usually deplorable conditions of their daily lives led them to seek this sort of escape? When welfare rolls rise dramatically, is it because more and more individual people are refusing to work, or could it be that the advancing technocracy has less need for unskilled and marginal labor?

You will recognize that the answers to these questions of social policy could be phrased in terms consistent either with personal attribution or with situational attribution. More importantly, the sort of attribution chosen will to a large degree determine the solutions proposed. Personal attributions about the reasons for welfare lead to political speeches about "welfare chiselers," appeals for return to simpler days of the Protestant ethic, and laws designed to make needed financial assistance more difficult to obtain. Situational attributions, on the other hand, are likely to suggest that expanded government-supported employment, better job training, and increased educational opportunity for all will provide more lasting reductions in public assistance.

Unfortunately, especially for the people who happen to be in the problem groups, overemphasis on personal causes is as common with social problems as it is with other more individual behaviors. It is not simply that behavior engulfs the field, or even that personal attributions for social problems are more satisfying to the perceivers. Social conditions are less accessible to influence and more resistant to constructive change than are individual people. At the most elementary level, people are more easily identified than are conditions. If you violate a law, you are a criminal by definition; if you are physically dependent upon a drug, you are an addict; if your income is below an established level, you are officially poor. There are no problems of interpretation, no differences of opinion among experts to deal with, no necessity for determining relative weightings of possible causes. All that is necessary is knowledge of the defining characteristic.

This emphasis upon personal attribution has the added advantage of specifying not only the problem, but also the solution: change the people. Punish the criminal (or remove him from society) and the crime problem will go away. Put all the addicts on methadone (an addictive synthetic drug which eliminates the craving for heroin and is usually administered by hospitals) and there will be no more addiction. Sterilize people on welfare and you will break the cycle of poverty. The most appealing aspect of this kind of approach is that it promises to correct the social problem by acting on the individual person. There is, however, some reason to believe that solutions to social problems based on correction of assumed personal dispositions will probably be futile. As long as the environmental conditions persist, they will probably lead to similar "personal dispositions" in other people. This sort of interaction between environmental conditions and personal dispositions can be illustrated, on an interpersonal rather than societal level, by the phenomenon of the self-fulfilling prophecy.

A Concluding Note: The Self-fulfilling Prophecy

An important aspect of the way in which our attributions affect our interpersonal behavior—which, in turn, affects our attributions—has been described by Merton (1957) as the *self-fulfilling prophecy*. This term refers to the fact that our expectations about an interaction can produce behavior on our part that will guarantee that the expectation is fulfilled. Let us consider some attributional examples. Suppose that you are a policeman in a large city and are in charge of maintaining order in the ghetto. You know that the crime rate is higher there than in any other part of the city, and in your patrols you frequently must deal with people behaving in a violent way. If we asked you to make an attribution for this violent behavior, you would probably say that it occurred "because they are just violent people." The result of this *personal* attribution is that you expect a violent response from anyone you stop, even for a routine traffic offense. The consequence? In order to establish your dominance at the beginning of the interaction, you, yourself, behave as violently as the laws and regulations permit. When you stop someone for a possible traffic violation, you approach the person's car with your gun drawn, you roughly pull the driver out of his seat, make him put his hands on top of the car, and only after you have thoroughly searched him do you ask to see his driver's license. If we pointed out to you that this is a pretty high-handed way to deal with the public, you would reply that your own behavior is dictated entirely by the *situation,* particularly by your attribution of potential violence to every individual living in the ghetto.

Now take the viewpoint of the ghetto resident. You know that to protect your family, to make sure that your child gets to school without losing his lunch money, to safeguard your few possessions, is to demonstrate your own willingness to take necessary revenge. In fact, perhaps the very best way to insure your family's safety in the harsh environment is to be known as a "bad dude" who had better be left alone. Your attribution for your own violent behavior would, therefore, be made entirely to the *situation.* It is not that you enjoy being tough, but rather that being so is the only way to survive in that environment. And what do you think of the police? They are an occupying force composed of individuals who enjoy throwing their weight around by hassling you and the people you know. Notice that this involves *personal* attributions of hostility to individual police officers. As Jones and Nisbett (1971) would say, each has emphasized the situational influences on his own behavior while emphasizing the importance of personal dispositions in producing the other's actions.

So what happens when the policeman (who attributes his own toughness to the situation, but attributes a disposition of violence to each resident) arrests a ghetto resident (who sees his own behavior as determined by the situation, but views the policeman's toughness as the product of a personal disposition)? Each one is likely to act in a way that will lead to a response by the other which confirms the incorrect attributions. The policeman may be arrogant and overly rough (leading the resident to fight back to protect himself), or the resident may be abusive and threatening (leading the policeman to be rough in order to protect himself). Each one obtains the expected response, and neither realizes that it is his own behavior at the time which produces that response. Each one's behavior fulfills the other's prophecy and strengthens the other's incorrect attribution for the causes of that behavior. The only way out of this situation is to provide an opportunity for police and residents to meet on neutral territory, under conditions that are designed to help both discover the mistaken attributions that they are making. If each can be made to realize that the other's violence is produced by the situation, rather than by a personal disposition, their adversary relationship might cool a great deal.

In passing, it should be noted that an adversary relationship is not an essential prerequisite for self-fulfilling misattribution. Such misattribution may occur even when the formal social relationship between the parties is one of concern or caring. One of the best examples of this sort of misattribution can be found in mental hospitals. There are always stories about the back-ward patients whose condition seems to improve around a new ward attendant who, for some reason, has not been told just how disturbed the patients on that ward really are. In this instance, the attendant's lack of expectations is clearly reflected in the apparently improved behavior of the patients.

Of all the attributions made to mental patients, none is more important and potentially harmful than the initial attribution made upon admission to the hospital, particularly if the admission has not been by choice. If you are involuntarily committed to a mental hospital, the legal system has formally attributed to you a personal disposition of *mental disorder*, for which you need treatment. The great extent to which hospital staff are likely to rely on this attribution, without determining its actual validity, is indicated in a series of studies reported by Rosenhan (1973). He arranged to have a number of willing graduate students committed by a court to mental hospitals for a short time as part of their clinical training. Although the real patients soon recognized the students for what they were, the staff members continued to believe that they were patients. Indeed, some of the students had substantial difficulty in securing their release at the appropriate time. Given that I have already made a personal attribution of mental disorder to you, what am I likely to think when you tell me that you really are not crazy, that you are a graduate student in clincial psychology, and that you were involuntarily committed as part of your clinical training? My, my, what an interesting delusional system! Imagine, I say to my colleagues, he claims that he is a student who is in here for training.

As we have noted before, once an attribution of mental disorder has been made it is likely to persist, even after all of the behaviors that originally led to the attribution have vanished. Even if all of the psychologists and psychiatrists available assert that you have been "cured," I may still believe that some residue of the disposition remains, and I may misattribute your future eccentricities (actions that I would excuse or ignore in "normal" people) to a resurgence of the disorder. If we did not commonly make such attributions, why would employers want to know whether you have ever been hospitalized for a mental disorder (or to broaden the perspective, ever convicted of a crime)? Do they ask you if you have ever had appendicitis? And should you be hired, would you be treated as just another employee, or would you be expected to "do something crazy" (or criminal) at any moment? Will we, by our expectations, put you under sufficient strain to make our original misattribution self-fulfilling? These are questions that must be answered if we are ever to make real progress in returning patients (or prisoners) to a society that will permit them to achieve their full potential as individuals unencumbered by attributions of personal dispositions that no longer exist.

From the examples cited in this chapter, we can get some idea of the importance that attribution plays in our everyday lives. Our social behavior is based in large part upon our knowledge of the interpersonal world, and that knowledge is obtained through attribution processes. A thorough understanding of how these processes function—and how they may be in error—will help us to become more accurate perceivers of our own actions and of the behavior of other people.

REFERENCES

Adorno, T. W., Frenkel-Brunswik, E., Levinson, D. J., and Sanford, R. N. *The authoritarian personality.* New York: Harper & Row, 1951.

Allport, F. H. *Theories of perception and the concept of structure.* New York: Wiley, 1955.

Allport, F. H. *Pattern and growth in personality.* New York: Holt, Rinehart and Winston, 1961.

Anderson, N. H. Primacy effects in personality impression formation using a generalized order effect paradigm. *Journal of Personality and Social Psychology,* 1965, *2,* 1–9.

Anderson, N. H. Application of a linear-serial model to a personality-impression task using serial presentation. *Journal of Personality and Social Psychology,* 1968, *10,* 354–362.

Anderson, N. H. Cognitive algebra: Integration theory applied to social attribution. In L. Berkowitz (Ed.), *Advances in experimental social psychology.* Vol. 7. New York: Academic Press, 1974.

Anderson, N. H., and Hubert, S. Effects of concomitant verbal recall on order effects in personality impression formation. *Journal of Verbal Learning and Verbal Behavior,* 1963, *2,* 379–391.

Anscombe, G. E. M. *Intention.* London: Basil Blackwell, 1957.

Asch, S. E. Forming impressions of personality. *Journal of Abnormal and Social Psychology,* 1946, *41,* 258–290.

Battle, E. S., and Rotter, J. B. Children's feelings of personal control as related to social class and ethnic group. *Journal of Personality,* 1963, *31,* 482-490.

Bem, D. J. Self-perception: An altenative interpretation of cognitive dissonance phenomena. *Psychological Review,* 1967, *74,* 183–200.

Bem, D. J. Self-perception theory. In L. Berkowitz (Ed.), *Advances in experimental social psychology.* Vol. 6. New York: Academic Press, 1972.

Bieri, J. Complexity-simplicity as a personality variable in cognitive and preferential behavior. In D. W. Fiske and S. R. Maddi (Eds.), *Functions of varied experience.* Homewood, Ill.: Dorsey Press, 1961.

Bruner, J. S. Going beyond the information given. In J. S. Bruner, E. Brunswik, L. Festinger, F. Heider, K. F. Muenzinger, C. E. Osgood, and D. Rapaport (Eds.), *Contemporary approaches to cognition.* Cambridge, Mass.: Harvard University Press, 1957.

Bruner, J. S., and Goodman, C. C. Value and need as organizing factors in perception. *Journal of Abnormal and Social Psychology,* 1947, *42,* 33–44.

Brunswik, E. *Wahrnemung und Gegenstandweit.* Leipzig and Vienna: Deuticke, 1934.

Cannon, W. B. *Bodily changes in fear, hunger, and rage.* (2nd ed.). New York: Appleton, 1929.

Catell, R. B., and Wenig, P. W. Dynamic and cognitive factors controlling misperception. *Journal of Abnormal and Social Psychology,* 1952, *47,* 797–809.

Chaikin, A. L., and Darley, J. M., Jr. Victim or perpetrator: Defensive attribution of responsibility and the need for order and justice. *Journal of Personality and Social Psychology,* 1973, *25,* 268–275.

Christie, R. Authoritarianism re-examined. In R. Christie and M. Jahoda (Eds.), *Studies in the scope and method of "The Authoritarian Personality."* New York: Free Press, 1954.

Cline, V. B. Interpersonal perception. In B. A. Maher (Ed.), *Progress in experimental personality research.* Vol. 1. New York: Academic Press, 1964.

Coleman, J., Campbell, E., Hobson, C., McPortland, J., Mood, A., Weinfield, F., and York, R. *Equality of educational opportunity.* Superintendent of Documents, Catalog No. FS5, 238:38001. Washington, D.C.: United States Government Printing Office, 1966.

Cooley, C. H. *Human nature and the social order.* New York: Scribner's, 1902.

Cronbach, L. J. Processes affecting scores on "understanding of others" and "assumed similarity." *Psychological Bulletin,* 1955, *52,* 177–193.

deCharms, R. C. *Personal causation: The internal affective determinants of behavior.* New York: Academic Press, 1968.

Duval, S., and Wicklund, R. A. A theory of objective self-awareness. New York: Academic Press, 1972.

Eriksen, B. A., and Eriksen, C. W. *Perception and personality.* Morristown, N. J.: General Learning Press, 1972.

Fauconnet, P. *La Responsibilité.* Paris: Alcan, 1920.

Festinger, L. A theory of social comparison processes. *Human Relations,* 1954, *7,* 117–140.

Festinger, L. *A theory of cognitive dissonance.* Stanford, Calif.: Stanford University Press, 1957.

Festinger, L., and Carlsmith, J. M. Cognitive consequences of forced compliance. *Journal of Abnormal and Social Psychology,* 1959, *58,* 203–210.

Goffman, E. On cooling the mark out: Some aspects of adaptation to failure. *Psychiatry,* 1952, *15,* 451–463.

Goffman, E. *The presentation of self in everyday life.* Garden City, N.Y.: Doubleday, 1959.

Gordon, C. Self-conceptions: Configurations of content. In C. Gordon and K. J. Gergen (Eds.), *The self in social interaction.* Vol. 1. New York: Wiley, 1968.

Gordon, C., and Gergen, K. J. *The self in social interaction.* Vol. 1. New York: Wiley, 1968.

Gurin, P., Gurin, G., Lao, R. C., and Beattie, M. Internal-external control in the motivational dynamics of Negro youth. *Journal of Social Issues,* 1969, *25,* 29–53.

Heider, F. Social perception and phenomenal causality. *Psychological Review,* 1944, *51,* 358–374.

Heider, F. *The psychology of interpersonal relations.* New York: Wiley, 1958.

Heider, F., and Simmel, M. An experimental study of apparent behavior. *American Journal of Psychology,* 1944, *57,* 243–259.

Hersch, P. D., and Scheibe, K. E. Reliability and validity of internal-external control as a personality dimension. *Journal of Consulting Psychology,* 1967, *31,* 609–613.

Himmelfarb, S., and Senn, D. Forming impressions of social class: Two tests of an averaging model. *Journal of Personality and Social Psychology,* 1969, *12,* 38-51.

Hochberg, J. E., and Gleitman, H. Towards a reformulation of the perception-motivation dichotomy. In J. S. Bruner and D. Krech (Eds.), *Perception and personality: A symposium.* Durham: Duke University Press, 1950.

Howes, D. H., and Solomon, R. L. Visual duration threshold as a function of word probability. *Journal of Experimental Psychology,* 1950, *41,* 401–410.

James, W. *Psychology: The briefer course.* New York: Holt, 1892.

James, W., and Lange, G. C. *The emotions.* Baltimore: Williams & Wilkins, 1922.

Jones, E. E., and Davis, K. E. From acts to dispositions: The attribution process in person perception. In L. Berkowitz (Ed.), *Advances in experimental social psychology.* Vol. 2. New York: Academic Press, 1965.

Jones, E. E., Davis, K. E., and Gergen, K. J. Role playing variations and their informational value for person peception. *Journal of Abnormal and Social Psychology,* 1961, *63,* 302–310.

Jones, E. E., and deCharms, R. Changes in social perception as a function of the personal relevance of behavior. *Sociometry,* 1957, *20,* 75–85.

Jones, E. E., and Gerard, H. B. *Foundations of social psychology.* New York: Wiley, 1967.

Jones, E. E., and Harris, V. A. The attribution of attitudes. *Journal of Experimental Social Psychology,* 1967, *3,* 1–24.

Jones, E. E., and Nisbett, R. E. *The actor and the observer: Divergent perceptions of the causes of behavior.* Morristown, N. J.: General Learning Press, 1971.

Jones, E. E., Rock, L., Shaver, K. G., Goethals, G. R., and Ward, L. M. Pattern of performance and ability attribution: An unexpected primacy effect. *Journal of Personality and Social Psychology,* 1968, *10,* 317–340.

Jones, E. E., and Thibaut, J. W. Interaction goals as bases of inference in person perception. In R. Taguiri and L. Petrullo (Eds.), *Person perception and interpersonal behavior.* Stanford: Stanford University Press, 1958.

Katkovsky, W., Crandall, V. C., and Good, S. Parental antecedents of children's beliefs in internal-external control of reinforcements in intellectual achievement situations. *Child Development,* 1967, *88,* 765–776.

Kelley, H. H. The warm-cold variable in first impressions of persons. *Journal of Personality,* 1950, *18,* 431–439.

Kelley, H. H. Attribution theory in social psychology. In D. Levine (Ed.), *Nebraska Symposium on Motivation, 1967.* Vol. 15. Lincoln, Neb.: University of Nebraska Press, 1967.

Kelley, H. H. *Attribution in social interaction.* Morristown, N. J.: General Learning Press, 1971.

Kelley, H. H. *Causal schemata and the attribution process.* Morristown, N. J.: General Learning Press, 1972.

Kelley, H. H. The processes of causal attribution. *American Psychologist,* 1973, *28,* 107–128.

Kelly, G. A. *The psychology of personal constructs.* Vols. 1 and 2. New York: Norton, 1955.

Kelly, G. A. *A theory of personality: The psychology of personal constructs.* New York: Norton, 1963.

Kohlberg, L. The cognitive-developmental approach to socialization. In D. A. Goslin (Ed.), *Handbook of socialization theory and research.* Chicago: Rand McNally, 1969.

Kuhn, M. H., and McPartland, T. S. An empirical investigation of self-attitudes. *American Sociological Review,* 1954, *19,* 68–76.

Landy, D., and Aronson, E. The influence of the character of the criminal and his victim on the decisions of simulated jurors. *Journal of Experimental Social Psychology,* 1969, *5,* 141–152.

Lazarus, R. S. *Psychological stress and the coping process.* New York: McGraw-Hill, 1966.

Lefcourt, H., and Ladwig, G. The American Negro: A problem in expectancies. *Journal of Personality and Social Psychology,* 1965, *1,* 377–380.

Lepper, M. R., Greene, D., and Nisbett, R. E. Undermining children's intrinsic interest with extrinsic reward: A test of the "over-justification" hypothesis. *Journal of Personality and Social Psychology,* 1973, *28,* 129-137.

Lerner, M. J. The unjust consequences of the need to believe in a just world. Paper presented at the meeting of the American Psychological Association, New York, September 1966.

Lerner, M. J., and Matthews, G. Reactions to suffering of others under conditions of indirect responsibility. *Journal of Personality and Social Psychology,* 1967, *5,* 319–325.

Levine, R., Chein, I., and Murphy, G. The relation of the intensity of a need to the amount of perceptual distortion: A preliminary report. *Journal of Psychology,* 1942, *13,* 238–293.

Luchins, A. S. Experimental attempts to minimize the impact of first impressions. In C. E. Hovland (Ed.), *The order of presentation in persuasion.* New Haven: Yale University Press, 1957.

Lüscher, M. *The Lüscher color test.* Edited and translated by I. Scott. New York: Random House, 1969.

Maslow, A. *Motivation and personality.* New York: Harper & Row, 1954.

McArthur, L. A. The how and what of why: Some determinants and consequences of causal attribution. *Journal of Personality and Social Psychology,* 1972, *22,* 171–193.

McGhee, P., and Crandall, V. C. Beliefs in internal-external control of reinforcements and academic performance. *Child Development,* 1968, *39,* 91–102.

McGinnies, E. Emotionality and perceptual defense. *Psychological Review,* 1949, *56,* 244–251.

McGuire, W. J. Personality and susceptibility to social influence. In E. F. Borgatta and W. W. Lambert (Eds.), *Handbook of personality theory and research.* Chicago: Rand McNally, 1968.

McLuhan, M. *Understanding media: The extensions of man.* New York: McGraw-Hill, 1964.

Mead, G. H. *Mind, self, and society.* Chicago: University of Chicago Press, 1934.

Merton, R. *Social theory and social structure.* Glencoe, Ill.: Free Press, 1957.

Mill, J. S. *A system of logic: Ratiocinative and inductive.* New York: Harper, 1846.

Mischel, W. *Personality and assessment.* New York: Wiley, 1968.

Nisbett, R. E., and Caputo, G. C. Personality traits: Why other people do the things they do. Unpublished manuscript. Yale University, 1971.

Nisbett, R. E., and Schachter, S. Cognitive manipulation of pain. *Journal of Experimental Social Psychology,* 1966, *2,* 227–236.

Nisbett, R. E., and Valins, S. *Perceiving the causes of one's own behavior.* Morristown, N. J.: General Learning Press, 1971.

Norman, W. T. Toward an adequate taxonomy of personality attributes: Replicated factor structure in peer nomination personality ratings. *Journal of Abnormal and Social Psychology,* 1963, *66,* 574–583.

Oden, G. C., and Anderson, N. H. Differential weighting in integration theory. *Journal of Experimental Psychology,* 1971, *89,* 152–164.

Orne, M. T. On the social psychology of the psychological experiment: With particular reference to demand characteristics and their implications. *American Psychologist,* 1962, *17,* 776–783.

Passini, F. T., and Norman, W. T. A universal conception of personality structure? *Journal of Personality and Social Psychology,* 1966, *4,* 44–49.

Piaget, J. *The moral judgment of the child.* London: Paul, Trench, Trubner, 1932.

Postman, L., Bruner, J. W., and McGinnies, E. Personal values as selective factors in perception. *Journal of Abnormal and Social Psychology,* 1948, *43,* 142–154.

Rokeach, M. *The open and closed mind.* New York: Basic Books, 1960.

Rokeach, M., and Vidmar, N. Testimony concerning possible jury bias in a Black Panther murder trial. *Journal of Applied Social Psychology,* 1973, *3,* 19–29.

Rosenhan, D. On being sane in an insane place. *Science,* 1973, *179,* No. 4070.

Ross, L. D., Rodin, J., and Zimbardo, P. G. Toward an attribution therapy: The reduction of fear through induced cognitive-emotional misattribution. *Journal of Personality and Social Psychology,* 1969, *12,* 279–288.

Rotter, J. B. *Social learning and clinical psychology.* Englewood Cliffs, N. J.: Prentice-Hall, 1954.

Rotter, J. B. Generalized expectancies for internal versus external control of reinforcement. *Psychological Monographs*, 1966, *80*, 1–28.

Ryle, G. *The concept of mind.* London: Hutchinson, 1949.

Schachter, S. The interaction of cognitive and physiological determinants of emotional state. In L. Berkowitz (Ed.), *Advances in experimental social psychology*. Vol. 1. New York: Academic Press, 1964.

Schachter, S., and Singer, J. E. Cognitive, social, and physiological determinants of emotional state. *Psychological Review,* 1962, *69,* 379–399.

Schaefer, E., and Murphy, G. The role of autism in a visual figure-ground relationship. *Journal of Experimental Psychology,* 1943, *32,* 335–343.

Shaver, K. G. Defensive attribution: Effects of severity and relevance on the responsibility assigned for an accident. *Journal of Personality and Social Psychology,* 1970, *14,* 101–113.

Shaver, K. G., Turnbull, A. A., and Sterling, M. P. Defensive attribution: The effects of occupational dangers and locus of control; perceiver sex and self-esteem. *Journal Supplement Abstract Service Catalog of Selected Documents in Psychology,* 1973, *3,* 48.

Shaw, M. E., and Sulzer, J. L. An empirical test of Heider's levels in attribution of responsibility. *Journal of Abnormal and Social Psychology,* 1964, *69,* 39–46.

Storms, M. D., and Nisbett, R. E. Insomnia and the attribution process. *Journal of Personality and Social Psychology*, 1970, *16*, 319-328.

Stotland, E., Sherman, S., and Shaver, K. G. *Empathy and birth order: Some experimental explorations.* Lincoln, Neb.: University of Nebraska Press, 1971.

Sulzer, J. L. Heider's "Levels Model" of responsibility attribution. Paper presented at the Symposium on Attribution of Responsibility Research, Williamsburg, Va., July 1971.

Taguiri, R. Person perception. In G. Lindzey and E. Aronson (Eds.), *Handbook of social psychology.* (2nd ed.). Vol. 3. Reading, Mass.: Addison-Wesley, 1969.

Taguiri, R., and Petrullo, L. *Person perception and interpersonal behavior.* Stanford, Calif.: Stanford University Press, 1958.

Thurstone, L. L. *Multiple factor analysis.* Chicago: University of Chicago Press, 1947.

Valins, S. Cognitive effects of false heart-rate feedback. *Journal of Personality and Social Psychology,* 1966, *4,* 400–408.

Valins, S., and Ray, A. A. Effects of cognitive desensitization on avoidance behavior. *Journal of Personality and Social Psychology,* 1967, *7,* 345–350.

Walster, E. Assignment of responsibility for an accident. *Journal of Personality and Social Psychology,* 1966, *3,* 73–79.

Weiner, B., Freize, I., Kukla, A., Reed, L., Rest, S., and Rosenbaum, R. M. *Perceiving the causes of success and failure.* Morristown, N. J.: General Learning Press, 1971.

Wheeler, L. *Interpersonal influence.* New York: Allyn & Bacon, 1970.

White, R. K. *Nobody wanted war: Misperception in Vietnam and other wars.* Garden City, N.Y.: Doubleday, 1970.

INDEX

Attribution theory *(continued)*
  determinism, 28, 57, 58
  origin, 9, 35, 36
Attribution therapy, 88, 89, 130,
  131. *See also* Misattribution
  therapy
Attributional criteria
  consensus, 52, 53, 55, 63, 64, 98,
    100, 128, 129
  consistency, 52, 53, 55, 63, 64, 98,
    100, 127
  distinctiveness, 52–54, 63, 64, 98,
    100, 127, 129
Attributional data table, 51, 54

Battle, E. S., 90, 139
Beattie, M., 91, 141
Behavior
  in-role, 50, 98, 119
  inferring attitudes, 82–89
  out-of-role, 50, 98, 119
  tendency to engulf the field, 38,
    82, 117, 118, 132
Behavior modification, 130, 131
Bem, D. J., 74, 82, 83, 85–87, 89,
  117, 139
Biases in attribution, 24–26, 39, 49,
  50, 55, 102, 106–110, 126. *See
  also* Errors in attribution
Bieri, J., 24, 140
Blacks
  attributions to police, 135, 136
  jury bias against, 4
  and locus of control, 90
Blameworthiness
  avoidance, 110
  as moral accountability, 101–103
Bruner, J. S., 13, 14, 23, 25, 140,
  144
Brunswik, E., 10, 11, 140

Campbell, E., 90, 140
Can
  as necessary condition for action,
    41
Cannon, W. B., 86, 140
Caputo, G. C., 122, 144
Carlsmith, J. M., 83, 84, 141

Categorization, 4, 13–15
Category mistake, 69, 70, 76, 119,
  120
Cattell, R. B., 25, 140
Causality, 43
  attributions, 3, 6
  category mistake in attribution,
    120
  dimensions, 94, 95
  phenomenal, 36–38
  and principle of covariation, 97,
    100
Causes
  facilitative, 98, 99
  inhibitory, 98, 99
  multiple necessary, 99, 100
  multiple sufficient, 99, 100
Chaikin, A. L., 110, 140
Chein, I., 25, 143
Children
  causality judgments, 38
  intrinsic motivation, 85, 86
  moral judgments, 101, 102
Choice circles, 45, 46
Christie, R., 23, 140
Cline, V. B., 22, 140
Cognition, compared to motivation,
  82, 86, 102
Cognitive complexity, 24
Cognitive consistency, 83
Cognitive dissonance, 83–86
Coleman, J., 90, 140
Commitment to mental hospitals,
  attributional effects, 70, 136,
  137
Components of action, personal
  and environmental, 39–42,
  60–63
Consensus, 52, 55, 64. *See also* Attributional criteria
Consistency, 52, 55, 63, 64. *See also*
  Attributional criteria
Constructive process, 10, 11
Context of action, 63–65
  importance in attribution, 55
Cooley, C. H., 27, 77, 140
Correspondence of inference, 48,
  49